FLY PATTERNS OF
ALASKA

ALASKA FLYFISHERS

REVISED AND ENLARGED EDITION

Editor
Dirk V. Derksen

Fly Photographer
Michael D. Scarbrough

FRANK AMATO PUBLICATIONS
PORTLAND, OREGON

Acknowledgments

In the decade since *Fly Patterns of Alaska* was first published, there has been a significant increase in fly fishing in Alaska's streams, lakes and oceans. Patterns have evolved and new flies developed as fly fishers have discovered new materials and better ways to simulate items in the diet of salmon, trout, char, grayling, sheefish, northern pike, and even halibut. As a result, we have nearly doubled the number of patterns illustrated in this new edition. Revision of *Fly Patterns of Alaska* required over two years of work and involved many members of the Alaska Flyfishers who contributed time and talent.

Patterns that appeared in the original work were donated to The American Museum of Fly Fishing. Each was retied for this revised edition by Dan Jordan, Russell King, or Dave Mitson. We thank all those members and former members of the Alaska Flyfishers who submitted patterns, recipes, and information about flies that first appeared in the 1983 volume and are now reprinted here along with 114 new patterns.

Individuals who contributed new flies, recipes, and background data for this revised edition include: Chuck Ash, Ed Atwell, Jim Cariello, Richard DeLorenzo, Dirk Derksen, Tony Frascarelli, T. Daniel Gillen, Keith Goltz, Greg Harrington, Selim Hassan, Jim Hemming, Richard Johnson, Marty Karstetter, Russell King, John Lewis, Dennis McAfee, Gary Miller, Dave Mitson, Bob Moss, Wayne Mushrush, Norval Netsch, Hank Pennington, Doug Rader, David Ragsdale, Mike Robinson, Dave Sullivan, Bruce Susinger, Dave Van Tuyl, Darrell Winter, Dennis Wood, and Paul Woodward.

The Alaska Flyfishers also thank Carol Goltz, Al Jacobs, Shirley Jacobs, Dick Evans, Bill LeLake, Eric Paule, and John P. Rogers for their care in proofreading various drafts of this volume--they helped improve it considerably.

CONTENTS

Working Committee
Howard Atchley, Keith Goltz, Richard Johnson, Dan Jordan (Chair), Russell King, Bob Merrill, Dave Mitson, & Paul Woodward

Front Cover photo: A floatplane maneuvers through the rugged peaks of the Chugach Mountains. Cary Anderson

Front Cover inset: Spey Day. Michael Scarbrough

Back Cover photo: North America's tallest peak, Mt. McKinley, at 20,320 feet presides over the surrounding landscape. Michael Scarbrough

Back Cover inset: Improved Sofa Pillow. Michael Scarbrough

First Page photo: Alaska's Arctic Valley is illuminated by this display of northern lights. Cary Anderson

Frontispiece photo: Lake Grosvenor in Katmai National Park. Michael Scarbrough

All other photo credits on page 80

Softbound ISBN: 1-878175-31-9
Hardbound ISBN: 1-878175-32-7
Printed in Hong Kong

10 9 8 7 6 5

Preface

Alaska. The name remains synonymous with wilderness so vast that grizzly bears and wolves live without human intrusion, where salmon can weigh a hundred pounds, and where trout as long as your leg can be caught on every cast. These are but a few of the bigger-than-life promises the 49th state makes to the world. "Come and enjoy our treasures," say the sourdoughs, "we are your best hope that future generations will be as blessed as you."

Since its formation in 1973, the Alaska Flyfishers has been at the front lines of the conservation battles fought to maintain the pristine quality of their fishing. When the Alaska Department of Fish & Game wanted to release 5,000 steelhead smolts in the Kenai Peninsula's Anchor River, the Alaska Flyfishers convincingly argued that the plants would have a negative impact on the wild stocks. The project was abandoned and a Steelhead Planning Team that included Dick Evans of the Alaska Flyfishers was formed. Club members remain vigilant—custodians of their wild steelhead populations.

The Alaska Flyfishers participated in the development of the Alaska Board of Fisheries *Cook Inlet & Copper River Basin Rainbow/Steelhead Trout Management Policy*, with club member Keith Goltz serving on the planning team. Rainbow trout would be managed at historical size, age, and stock levels. More recently, the Alaska Flyfishers campaigned to have sections of the upper Kenai River set aside as a world-class catch-and-release rainbow trout fishery.

Locking horns with the state's politics and policies has not robbed the Alaska Flyfishers of their vitality and good humor. Membership continues to grow and now stands at nearly 500. Fly fishing seminars, an annual donation of $1000 to the Anchorage public library for fishing books and videos, club outings, and the club newsletter, *FlyLines*, keeps club goals in common with community aspirations.

The bright edge of these many good works is this book, *Fly Patterns of Alaska*. I purchased my copy when it was initially published in 1983, and for the first time my fellow fly fishers and I gained a coherent picture of Alaska's astonishingly varied angling wealth: steelhead, rainbows, Arctic char, Dolly Varden, grayling, and five species of salmon. The book began with the Alaska Mary Ann, the State's first homeborn pattern and, incidentally, the fly at the center of the club's logo. The reader was then led to such local favorites as the Katmai Smolt, Kenai Connection, and Arctic Shrew, 129 fly entries in all.

The revised edition offers 251 patterns drawn from a network of guides, local experts, and lodge owners throughout the state. This wealth of information is arranged in six categories, including an entire chapter on salt water. New flies are intended for still more gamefish, including the legendary sheefish, lake trout, northern pike, even the Pacific halibut. A brief commentary explains where a pattern has been most effective, and how it is best fished. Dirk Derksen, the editor of this book, explained, "We have considered everything, from midges to mice!"

The scope of *Fly Patterns of Alaska* has kept pace with the rapidly expanding sport of fly fishing, Alaska style. A new generation of anglers can read this book, tie its flies, and venture north to search for the trophy gamefish of their dreams. Thanks in no small measure to the leadership provided by the Alaska Flyfishers, their quest will be successful.

-Trey Combs
Port Townsend, Washington
July 15, 1992

The Alaska Flyfishers:
An Action Company of Anglers

Keith Goltz

The formation of any organization, including an angling organization, involves a certain degree of risk. As Ralph Waldo Emerson points out, "one may take a good deal of pains to bring people together, and to organize clubs and debating societies, and yet no result come of it." Fortunately, when the Alaska Flyfishers came together they stayed together—and much that was good came of that.

Coming Together

The Alaska Flyfishers first came together on February 26, 1973. The meeting was held in a basement classroom at the old Anchorage Gymnasium—it drew 35 people. By the end of March the Club had officers, by-laws and a newsletter; by the end of its first year, its membership roster had grown to over 100.

Officially, the Club was formed "to improve and increase the sport of fly fishing in Alaska," especially fly fishing for trout. It adopted the Alaska Mary Ann—a streamer derived from an Eskimo lure—as its official Club fly. And it resolved that meetings should be simple affairs, conducted according to the "rules of common courtesy among fly fishermen."

This resolve was made by individuals of a single mind; individuals captivated by the prospect of applying the arts of fly fishing to the rich and varied waters of Alaska. Predictably,

their enthusiasm could not be contained. It had to be shared with others.

Teaching Others

In the spring of 1974, the Alaska Flyfishers conducted its first fly fishing seminar. In succeeding years it has devoted four consecutive Mondays in April to the teaching of fly fishing fundamentals. Now in its 20th year, more than 2,000 Alaskans have participated in at least one of the seminar functions.

Traditionally, the first session of the seminar is devoted to basic equipment, including: rods and reels, lines and leaders, vests and waders, vises and threads. Following sessions deal with flies and fly tying, fishing tactics, and fly casting. Over much of its history, the Club has used Sheridan Anderson's *Curtis Creek Manifesto* as its training text. Recently, the Flyfishers completed their own text—a fly fishing primer keyed to the waters of Alaska.

Club Outings

When the seminar is over—and sometimes before—the Alaska Flyfishers look to their home waters. There's a lot to look at: 3,000 rivers; 3,000,000 (yes, Minnesota, that's *three million*) freshwater lakes; plus 33,000 miles of saltwater coast. While these waters are most often fished by twos and by threes, sometimes the groups are much larger.

Over the years a couple of these groupings have become habitual. In May, the Club gathers at Matanuska Lake to pursue trout and to exercise its float tubing skills. In June, it gathers around the Middle Russian River to exercise some of the Kenai Peninsula's wild and healthy rainbows.

Conservation Projects

Of course, most healthy fisheries do not "just happen"—they require keeping and tending. In Alaska, as elsewhere, much of the tending is done in fisheries close to population centers. So it is that the Club's most visible conservation project—the bank stabilization at Campbell Creek—is done squarely within Anchorage, the largest city in the state.

There are other projects too: projects less visible; projects just as important. For example, the Club was actively represented on the Cook Inlet Sport Fishing Team that assisted the Alaska Department of Fish and Game in the development of the *Cook Inlet Rainbow/Steelhead Trout Management Policy*. In addition, the Club assigned one of its members to the Kenai Peninsula Steelhead Planning Team that advised the Department on management of steelhead in the Anchor and Ninilchik rivers as well as in Deep and Stariski creeks.

Scheduled Meetings

The status of these projects is reported during the Club's regular monthly meetings. For the most part, these meetings center on a fisheries presentation. Often, the presentations are made by professional biologists from the Alaska Department of Fish and Game or the U. S. Fish and Wildlife Service; at other times, the presentations are made by ordinary fishermen—usually from Alaska, sometimes from the "lower 48."

In addition to monthly meetings, special meetings are scheduled on a regular basis. In winter these special sessions focus on fly tying; in summer the sessions (usually held at Jewel Lake Park) focus on fly casting. Since over 100 of the Club's 525 memberships are now family memberships, most of these meetings have a definite "family" cant to them.

Alaska Flylines

Notice of all Club activity is given in *FlyLines*, the monthly newsletter of the Alaska Flyfishers. In the early days, the newsletter was mostly just a meeting fact sheet—pulled together the night before (sometimes the night after) the mailing deadline. In recent years, it has become much more.

In addition to Club news and conservation reports, *FlyLines* now carries articles on the tying of Alaska flies and the fishing of Alaska's waters. In-state, *FlyLines* goes out to members in 27 different communities—from Barrow (high on the Arctic plain) to Juneau (on the forested shores of Southeast). It is also mailed outside of Alaska, to Club members in 17 different states and three foreign countries.

Loussac Library

Obviously, the literary heritage of fly fishing extends far beyond newsletters—over the past 400 years or so, more writing has been devoted to fishing than to any other single branch of the sporting world. In order to make more of this writing accessible locally, the Alaska Flyfishers has donated its dollars and its energies toward enriching the collections of the Anchorage public libraries. After the new $43 million Z. J. Loussac Library was dedicated, in 1986, the Club prepared an annotated bibliography of the library's sportfishing collection; at that point, the Club had donated 30% of the titles.

Since that time the percentage has increased. Lately, the Alaska Flyfishers have given over $1000.00 a year to enhance the library's holdings of both books and videotapes. At the top of Loussac's large staircase, the City of Anchorage has placed a bronze plaque which (along with others) publicly acknowledges the contributions the Flyfishers have made to the public's library system.

Pattern Book

In the early 1980's, the Club undertook a writing of its own. While much that was being written of Alaska's fly fishing was entertaining, much of it was also "inaccurate and fragmented." So it was that in 1983 the Alaska Flyfishers published *Fly Patterns of Alaska*, a book designed to "present a selection of fly patterns that are particularly effective in Alaskan waters."

In its first printing *Fly Patterns* was a sellout; it was reprinted in 1985. Since that time the public's interest in fly fishing has grown substantially, as has the number of Alaska fly patterns. In this, its second edition, *Fly Patterns* nearly doubles the number of flies and fly recipes.

In addition, it increases the variety of color plates and adds more than a dozen reference charts linking individual flies with specific species of Alaska's sport fish. The flies used as models for the second edition will be donated (as they were for the first edition) to The American Museum of Fly Fishing. Proceeds from the book will again be used to support Club activities.

In all likelihood, there will be lots of activites to support. While in many (perhaps most) respects the Alaska Flyfishers are just like anglers world-wide, they do retain a substantial touch of Alaska's frontier spirit—they like to make things happen. And, if the future is anything at all like the past, much that is good will come of that.

Streamers and Bucktails

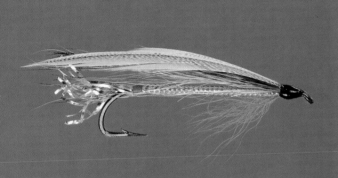

ALASKA MARY ANN

Hook: *Partridge CS17, sizes 4-6*
Thread: *Black*
Tail: *Red hackle fibers*
Body: *Ivory or light tan floss*
Ribbing: *Medium flat silver tinsel*
Wing: *White polar bear hair*
Cheeks: *Jungle cock (optional)*
Tying tip: *Bucktail or goat hair may be substituted for polar bear wing.*

This is the official fly of the Alaska Flyfishers. It was developed by Frank Dufresne, and several versions of the story about its origin exist. Even Dufresne himself has been reported to have told different stories on different occasions. For many years Eskimo women in the Kotzebue area have used a small jig, called the "Kobuk Hook," to jig for char and sheefish through the ice. It is made from a sliver of ivory, a bent and sharpened nail, and some polar bear hair. Dufresne tried them on a fly rod and found them very effective. When he ran out of the originals, he tied a duplicate using regular fly tying materials.

According to one story, the fly was named for the Eskimo lady who gave Dufresne the "Kobuk Hooks" and whose name was Mary Ann. This version was shown to club member Harry Geron in 1953 at Sparrevohn Air Force Station by a man who claimed to have been a friend of Dufresne, who showed him how to tie it and told him its history. For many years this has been a good pattern for virtually all predatory fish in Alaskan rivers and lakes.

ALASKAN SMOLT

Hook: *Mustad 9575, sizes 2-6*
Thread: *Black*
Tail: *Silver mylar tubing extending from body, unraveled*
Body: *Silver mylar tubing tied at rear with fluorescent orange*
thread, weighted
Throat: *Red calf tail*
Wing: *White bucktail, over which is tied brown bucktail dyed green*
Topping: *Mallard flank*

Originated by Bud Hodson for rainbows, salmon, and char in the Bristol Bay area. This fly is effective wherever salmon smolt are common prey.

BLACK GHOST STREAMER

Hook: *Tiemco 300, sizes 2-6*
Thread: *Black*
Tail: *Yellow hackle fibers*
Body: *Black floss*
Ribbing: *Medium flat silver tinsel*
Throat: *Yellow hackle fibers*
Wing: *Four white saddle hackles*
Cheeks: *Jungle cock (optional)*

The Black Ghost was originated in 1927 by Herbert L. Welsh of Mooselookmeguntic, Maine. Fred Babcock, past president of the Alaska Flyfishers, discovered the value of this classic streamer for rainbow trout and salmon in area lakes and streams.

BLACK MARABOU MUDDLER

Hook: *Tiemco 5263, sizes 2-8*
Thread: *Black*
Tail: *Red marabou*
Body: *Silver mylar tinsel chenille, weighted*
Wing: *Brown marabou over which is tied black marabou*
Collar: *Spun deer hair*
Head: *Spun deer hair, trimmed to shape*

Some professional guides in Alaska rate this fly as one of the best for trophy rainbows and grayling. Effective variations include wings of all-white, all-brown, or all-yellow marabou. This pattern should be fished deep. The movement of marabou can often entice big fish when nothing else will.

BLACK MATUKA

Hook: *Partridge CS17, sizes 2-6*
Thread: *Black*
Body: *Black wool, weighted*
Ribbing: *Oval silver tinsel*

Hackle: *Black webby neck hackle*
Wing: *Black webby neck hackle, tied Matuka style*

Large Black Matukas are excellent for large rainbows, Dolly Varden and trophy-size grayling. This pattern can be tied in many color variations, with all-black or all-brown the most popular.

BLACK NOSED DACE

Hook: *Tiemco 5263, sizes 2-8*
Thread: *Black*
Tail: *Red yarn*
Body: *Medium flat silver tinsel*
Ribbing: *Fine oval silver tinsel*

Wing: *Three layers: from bottom to top—white polar bear hair or bucktail, black bear hair, brown bucktail*
Tying tip: *Dress very sparse*

In Alaska, this pattern imitates salmon smolt and stickleback. The Black Nosed Dace is popular for Dolly Varden, pink salmon, and rainbow trout in streams or lakes.

BLUE SMOLT

Hook: *Mustad 9575, sizes 2-6*
Thread: *Black*
Tail: *Silver mylar tubing extended beyond body, unraveled*
Body: *Silver mylar tubing tied at rear with fluorescent orange*

thread, weighted
Throat: *Red calf tail*
Wing: *White bucktail over which is tied blue bucktail*
Topping: *Mallard flank feather, tied flat over wing*

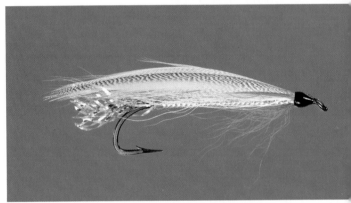

Bud Hodson claims credit for this popular trout and grayling pattern which is widely used in the Wood River, Tikchik Lakes, and Iliamna areas. Also, Phil Driver has found this pattern to be excellent for sheefish. Phil allows it to sink four to six feet and retrieves it with short jerks. Fishing for sheefish is best in estuaries, lakes, and river mouths right after the ice is out (usually June) in the Selawik and Kobuk rivers. Sheefish move farther inland in summer as they progress upstream to spawn. Phil has taken sheefish weighing over thirty pounds, but the usual size taken is 8 to fifteen pounds. Number 8- to 10- weight outfits are usually needed. An effective variation of this fly is one with a lavender wing section rather than the blue.

BUNNY WOOLHEAD SCULPIN

Hook: *Tiemco 7999, sizes 2/0-4*
Thread: *Black*
Tail: *Extension of rabbit fur strip used for body*
Body: *Cerise rabbit fur strip, wrap-*

ped over rear 2/3 of hook shank, weighted
Throat: *Flame Glo-Bug yarn (optional)*
Head: *Black wool clipped to shape*

Ed Sharpe of Wilderness Place Lodge first described this fly to Richard Johnson; Rich then tied it, adding the bright throat as a personal touch. Rich uses the fly throughout the season for stream rainbows and Dolly Varden. He fishes the fly in two basic ways: 1) with a floating line and a weighted leader, or 2) with a sink-tip line and a short leader.

COHO SPECTRUM

Hook: *Mustad 9575, sizes 2-6*
Thread: *Black*
Tail: *Mylar tubing extending from body, unraveled*
Body: *Silver mylar tubing tied at*

rear with fluorescent orange thread, weighted
Wing: *Four layers of bucktail: from bottom to top—white, green, blue, and black*

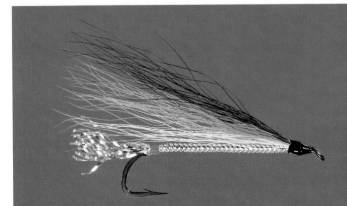

Originated by Bud Hodson, the Coho Spectrum is most effective for rainbow, Arctic char, Dolly Varden, and grayling in the spring when salmon smolt are migrating downstream.

CORONATION BUCKTAIL

Hook: *Partridge CS17, sizes 2-6*
Thread: *Black*
Body: *Medium flat silver tinsel*
Ribbing: *Medium oval or embossed silver tinsel*

Wing: *Three equal bunches of polar bear hair or bucktail: from bottom to top—white, red, and medium blue*

The Coronation was developed by a group of Puget Sound fishermen who originally used it when trolling for coho salmon. They dressed it on a 2/0 to 3/0 long-shanked hook with a ring eye. Tied on standard streamer hooks and fished as a smolt, the Coronation has proven to be effective for rainbows, grayling, and most salmon in Alaska.

DAVE'S FRY FLY NO. 1

Hook: *Partridge CS5, sizes 4-8*
Thread: *White*
Tail: *Mylar tubing extending from body, unraveled*
Body: *Pearlescent mylar tubing over white thread*
Wing: *White bucktail under, light brown bucktail over; narrow,*

dark grizzly hackle along each side
Eyes: *White with black pupil*
Tying tip: *Bucktail wing is pulled back Thunder Creek style and tied down with red thread to simulate gills*

Club member Dave Mitson began his "work-up" of this fly in 1977. The grizzly hackle was tied to simulate the parr marks of spring fry, and the pearlescent body was tied to simulate the flash of the fry as they move through the water column. Using a floating line, Mitson animates the fly with small darting actions. This is a fly that works in all seasons and all waters—wherever salmon fry are present.

GASTINEAU SMOLT

Hook: *Mustad 9575, sizes 4-12*
Threads: *White; red behind eyes*
Eyes: *Small bead chain*
Body: *Flat silver tinsel overwrapped with 10-12 pound test monofila-*

ment
Wing: *Brown bear hair topped by 5-10 strands of peacock Krystal Flash*

The Gastineau Smolt, patterned originally after the Humpy Fry Fly, has evolved into a more durable and more effective salmon smolt imitation. Fished in spring and early summer, the fly is effective for both stream rainbows and Dolly Varden. Norval Netsch, the fly's creator, uses a floating line retrieved with short and erratic strips.

GRAYBACK STREAMER

Hook: *Mustad 79580, size 6*
Thread: *Black*
Tail: *Natural deer body hair extended from body*
Body: *Olive chenille topped by*

natural deer body hair, weighted
Ribbing: *Copper wire*
Wing: *Furnace hackles*
Hackle: *Brown*

This fly comes from Roundup, Montana. An old-time Roundup tier, Tuck McCann, taught the tie to T. Daniel Gillen when Dan was only 12 years old. Dan uses it during the spring and fall seasons on the Kenai River and Deep Creek, fishing very close to the bottom with sinking lines.

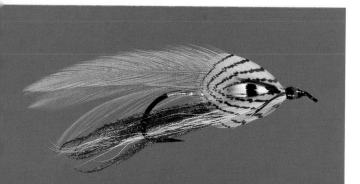

GRAY GHOST STREAMER

Hook: *Partridge CS17, sizes 2-6*
Thread: *Black*
Tag: *Narrow flat silver tinsel*
Body: *Orange floss*
Ribbing: *Narrow flat silver tinsel*
Throat: *Four or five peacock herl strands next to body, then white*

bucktail, then short golden pheasant crest
Wing: *Golden pheasant crest topped by four olive gray saddle hackles*
Shoulder: *Silver pheasant body feather*
Cheeks: *Jungle cock (optional)*

This important streamer was originated in 1924 by Mrs. Carrie Stevens to simulate smelt. In Alaska, this classic may represent a variety of forage fishes in the diet of salmon, trout, and char. It is a particularly good choice for lake trout. It can be cast or trolled.

HARRY'S SMOLT

Hook: *Mustad 9672, sizes 2-6*
Thread: *Black*
Tail: *Red hackle fibers*
Body: *Silver embossed tinsel*
Throat: *Red hackle fibers*
Wing: *Four blue hackle feathers*
Shoulder: *Gray-barred body feather*
Cheeks: *Jungle cock or substitute*

Harry Morrison designed and used this smolt imitation for rainbow trout and Dolly Varden from breakup (usually early April) to early June. Harry, who was a sport fishing guide on the Kenai River and a commercial fly tier, recommended this version for dark days and a variation with green wings for sunny days.

HYDE'S SCULPIN

Hook: *Mustad 7970, size 2*
Thread: *Black*
Tail: *Three layers: from bottom to top—yellow marabou, brown marabou, and brown Cree hackle*
Body: *Tan chenille*
Ribbing: *Gold oval tinsel*
Wing: *Fox squirrel topped by Cree hackle*
Fins: *Dyed mallard flank feathers trimmed to simulate pectoral fins*
Head: *Spun dark brown deer body hair trimmed to shape*

A creation of Ron Hyde that has proven effective for rainbow trout and silver salmon throughout Alaska, Hyde's Sculpin works best in slow water and in deep pools. Cast it slightly downstream and mend a little slack allowing the fly to sink. Then allow it to bounce along the bottom while retrieving it slowly using four- to six-inch strips. Ron has been a sport fishing guide in Alaska since 1970.

HYDE'S SINKING SCULPIN

Hook: *Mustad 7970, size 2*
Thread: *Black*
Tail: *Three layers: from bottom to top—yellow marabou, brown marabou, and brown Cree hackle*
Body: *Tan chenille*
Ribbing: *Gold oval tinsel*
Hackle: *Four mallard flank feathers dyed to simulate wood duck*
Wing: *Fox squirrel tail on bottom and Cree hackle on top*

This companion fly to Hyde's Sculpin is used in fast water for large rainbows and silver salmon. Casting across or quartering downstream and mending a little slack to allow the fly to sink quickly usually achieves the best results. Hyde's Sinking Sculpin is also effective for spot fishing in small holding pools and feeding stations behind rocks and logs.

KATMAI SMOLT

Hook: *Eagle Claw 1197G, sizes 4-8*
Thread: *Black*
Tail: *Light insect green floss*
Body: *Light insect green floss*
Butt: *Peacock herl*
Ribbing: *Peacock herl and fine oval silver tinsel*
Throat: *Mixed blue and red hackle fibers*
Wing: *Cream polar bear hair over which is tied light green bucktail*
Topping: *Five or six strands of peacock herl*
Cheeks: *Jungle cock (optional)*

Although many other patterns are more accurate imitations of salmon smolt, this Dan Flanders pattern has proven especially effective for large rainbows in the Katmai and Iliamna drainages. It has accounted for good catches of large rainbow in Dream and Gibralter creeks, and Flanders has used it successfully on the Brooks River as well as in lakes in southcentral Alaska.

KENAI CONNECTION

Hook: *Eagle Claw 1197G, sizes 1/0-6*
Thread: *Fluorescent chartreuse*
Tail: *Red hackle fibers*
Body: *Fluorescent chartreuse chenille*
Ribbing: *Gold tinsel*
Throat: *Red hackle fibers*
Wing: *White marabou*
Topping: *Peacock herl*
Cheeks: *Jungle cock (optional)*

Developed by Anchorage guide and outfitter Chris Goll for use on the Kenai River as a high visibility smolt and fry imitator, the Kenai Connection is particularly effective in milky, glacial waters. It has proven to be an excellent rainbow and char producer. It also works well on lake trout, steelhead, and salmon. Chris is a past President of the Alaska Flyfishers.

KIWI MUDDLER

Hook: *Tiemco 300, sizes 2-6*
Thread: *Brown*
Tail: *Pearlescent mylar tubing extending from body, unraveled*
Body: *Medium pearlescent mylar*

tubing, weighted
Wing: *Natural rabbit fur strip and pearlescent Flashabou*
Head: *Spun deer body hair trimmed to shape*

The Kiwi Muddler is a New Zealand pattern, featured on the Jack Dennis video: *Tying Western Trout Flies*. Wayne Mushrush uses the fly on Kenai River rainbows, as well as on char and rainbow trout in other areas. Wayne recommends that the fly be heavily weighted and fished right on the bottom, with a basic "muddler/sculpin" technique.

LABRADOR RETRIEVER

Hook: *Eagle Claw 1197G, sizes 4-8*
Thread: *Black*
Tail: *Red hackle fibers*
Body: *Peacock herl*
Ribbing: *Flat gold mylar tinsel*

Hackle: *Black*
Wing: *White polar bear hair or substitute*
Topping: *Five or six strands of peacock herl*

The prototype for this pattern came about at a fly tying demonstration where Dan Flanders was asked to demonstrate the dubbing technique. Lacking dubbing material, Dan looked around and noticed his old Labrador was snoozing under the table. Awakened, the dog put his head in his boss's lap for a patting. He was shedding at the time and a couple of good rubs collected enough material for dubbing a body on a large hook. The rest of the materials were scraps of what happened to be on the tying bench. The fly looked good and a few more were tied for field testing. Smaller sizes, 6 and 8, were very effective for rainbows migrating upstream in upper Montana Creek just after the anchor ice had gone out. The old Lab has since gone on to his reward and peacock herl is substituted for the dubbed body. This is also a good pattern in lakes and should be effective for steelhead and char.

LAKE LEECH

Hook: *Tiemco 5263, sizes 6-10*
Thread: *Color to match body*
Tail: *Tips of marabou that form body*

Body: *Purple marabou wrapped around weighted hook*
Tying tip: *Black, olive, and white are also good colors*

The Lake Leech represents a food item common to the lakes of Alaska. Darrell Winter, a former Club president, fishes the fly from his float tube—either with a slow bouncing retrieve or on a slow troll. Some Club members claim that this simple fly, tied in a variety of colors, is fully as effective as its larger and better known cousin—the ubiquitous Woolly Bugger.

LITTLE CHINOOK

Hook: *Mustad 9575, sizes 2-6*
Thread: *Black*
Tail: *Silver mylar tubing extended from body, unraveled*
Body: *Silver mylar tubing, tied at rear with fluorescent orange thread, weighted*

Throat: *Red hackle fibers*
Wing: *Silver mylar tubing, unraveled, topped by white marabou with light blue-dyed grizzly hackle on each side*
Topping: *Peacock herl*

Ron Clauson originated this chinook (king) salmon juvenile imitation while guiding on the Nushagak River. It is especially good for rainbow, large grayling, Dolly Varden, and Arctic char.

LITTLE RAINBOW TROUT

Hook: *Partridge CS17, sizes 4-12*
Thread: *Black*
Tail: *Green bucktail*
Body: *Mixed white and pink goat underfur or dubbing substitute*
Ribbing: *Flat silver tinsel*

Throat: *Red or pink calf tail*
Wing: *Small bunches of bucktail in three layers: from bottom to top—white, pink, and green*
Topping: *Natural brown bucktail*
Cheeks: *Jungle cock (optional)*

Dirk Derksen of Anchorage ties this version and finds it most effective in sizes 4 and 6, fished near the bottom in clear water streams of the Alaska Peninsula and southcentral Alaska. It can be fished either in dead drift or retrieved with short jerks. This is a good attractor for rainbow trout.

LORRAINE'S LAKE CREEK SMOLT

Hook: *Mustad 9575, sizes 2-8*
Thread: *Black*
Tail: *Red wool yarn*
Body: *Silver mylar tubing tied at rear with fluorescent orange thread, over lead wire*

Throat: *Yellow hackle fibers*
Wing: *Polar bear hair, or substitute, over which is tied brown bear hair*
Topping: *Six strands of peacock herl*

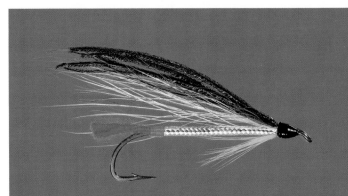

This pattern was originated by Ron Clauson while fishing on Lake Creek at Martana Lodge, approximately 100 air miles northwest of Anchorage. Size 6 is quite effective on large grayling, and sizes 2 and 4 are good for rainbows during the salmon smolt migration in the spring.

McNALLY MAGNUM

Hook: *Mustad 36717, sizes 1/0-2*
Thread: *Black*
Body: *Yellow chenille*
Wing: *Two or three yellow saddle*

hackles tied on each side and flared outward
Hackle: *Red*

Fred Babcock learned of the McNally Magnum from an article written by Ronald N. Dalby in the *Alaskafest* magazine. The article described the effectiveness of this pattern for northern pike. Fred tied a half dozen flies and sent them to a friend to try. Fred's friend gave them a try but reported little luck for pike. However, he did have great success for lake trout in the Delta Junction area. Later reports do confirm the effectiveness of this pattern for northern pike, which abound in many areas in Alaska.

MICKEY FINN BUCKTAIL

Hook: *Tiemco 5263, sizes 2-8*
Thread: *Black*
Body: *Medium flat silver tinsel*
Ribbing: *Narrow oval silver tinsel*
Wing: *Three layers of bucktail: from*

bottom to top—yellow, red, and yellow
Tying tip: *Make small bunches of bucktail to reduce bulk and size of head*

Originally known as the Red and Yellow Bucktail, this venerable pattern was popularized in the writings of John A. Knight. The Mickey Finn is a widely used streamer in Alaska, where it is an excellent standby for rainbows, steelhead, Dolly Varden, cutthroat, and salmon.

MOFO MUDDLER

Hook: *Tiemco 7999, sizes 2-6*
Thread: *Black*
Tag: *Silver tinsel and yellow floss*
Tail: *Black bucktail over golden pheasant crest*
Butt: *Black ostrich*
Body: *Gold mylar tubing, wound around hook*
Wing: *Black bear hair*
Topping: *Peacock sword and golden*

pheasant crest
Cheeks: *Jungle cock (optional)*
Head: *Spun deer body hair—rear is black and front is white, clipped to shape*
Tying Tip: *A short monofilament loop is tied into the head and secured to the shank prior to spinning the deer hair.*

Ken Mears of Anchorage developed this unusual Muddler version that is fished in an unorthodox style. To fish this fly, thread your leader through the loop of monofilament, then tie it to the eye of the hook. It should be fished on the surface downstream to produce a wake in the water. It is particularly effective on big water on the Alaska Peninsula for large rainbow. It will cause fish to rise and strike when traditional quick-sinking Alaskan patterns fail.

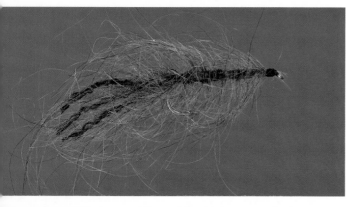

MOHAIR LEECH

Hook: *Tiemco 5263, sizes 6-8*
Thread: *Black*
Tail: *Mohair yarn to match color of*

body
Body: *Canadian brown mohair yarn; pick out fibers*

The Mohair Leech was developed by Club member Richard Johnson through the time honored (and inevitable) process of trial-and-error. The fly is designed to be fished—very slowly—near the surface and over the top of weed beds. Rich uses the fly on both the trout and grayling of Alaska's southcentral lakes.

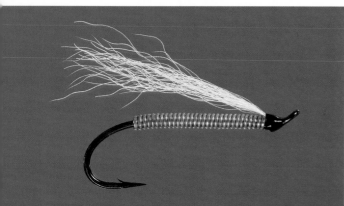

MONTANA BRASSY

Hook: *Tiemco 7999, sizes 10-14*
Thread: *Black*

Body: *Copper wire*
Wing: *White bucktail*

Sam Virgilleo of Westchester, Pennsylvania, taught Phil Brna to tie this pattern. Phil has used this fly in Alaska to take rainbow, grayling, Dolly Varden, steelhead, silver and red salmon. This pattern can be fished dead drift or retrieved as a conventional streamer. In small sizes it can be fished like a nymph. The Brassy can be tied in various sizes and wing colors, but white wings have always been most effective for Phil.

FLY PATTERNS OF ALASKA

MORRISON'S SECRET

Hook: *Mustad 36717, sizes 2-6*
Thread: *Black*
Tail: *Golden pheasant tippets*
Body: *Silver mylar piping wound around hook*
Hackle: *Red*
Wing: *White polar bear hair or substitute over which is tied green-dyed polar bear hair*
Topping: *Four to seven strands of peacock herl*
Eyes: *Large silver bead chain*

Harry Morrison caught a 28-inch rainbow in 1975 on the very first cast ever made with this fly. It has continued to be very effective for rainbows when fished with a fast retrieve. It is also good for Dolly Varden, lake trout, silver, red, and pink salmon, and steelhead on the Kenai Peninsula and in southeast Alaska. Harry designed this fly to resemble candle fish (Eulachon), which are forage for salmon in saltwater, and to imitate juvenile salmon that are fed upon by large rainbows and Dolly Varden in freshwater. An effective variation is to substitute blue polar bear hair for the green in the wings.

MOSSBACK MUDDLER MINNOW

Hook: *Tiemco 300, sizes 2-8*
Thread: *Olive*
Tail: *Peacock sword*
Body: *Green Diamond Braid*
Thorax: *Spun olive deer body hair*
Wing: *Olive marabou topped by peacock sword*
Head: *Spun olive deer body hair trimmed to shape*

David Ragsdale first tied this variation of the muddler in the winter of 1989. He tested it the following spring and has since scored numerous rainbows on Kenai Peninsula and Matanuska/Susitna Valley streams.

MUDDLER MINNOW

Hook: *Tiemco 300, sizes 2-8*
Thread: *Tan*
Tail: *Mottled turkey quill segment*
Body: *Gold tinsel*
Wing: *Underwing of gray squirrel tail; overwing of paired segments of mottled turkey quill*
Head: *Spun deer body hair trimmed to shape*

A pattern that is deadly all over the world for many species, the Muddler is effective in Alaska for everything from grayling to chinook salmon and is usually fished deep. This gold-bodied version is a favorite in clear water, and a silver-bodied version is useful in more turbid or glacial waters.

PARR FLY

Hook: *Mustad 9672, sizes 2-10*
Thread: *Tan, olive, or gray*
Body: *Oval gold tinsel*
Throat: *Blue dun-dyed bucktail*
Wing: *Brown hairs from a blue dun-dyed bucktail; grizzly hackles along sides to simulate parr marks*
Topping: *Four to five strands of pearl Krystal Flash*
Eyes: *Painted yellow with black pupil*

While research diving in Alaska streams, Hank Pennington noticed that the two most dominant features of small fry are their eyes and their parr markings. The Parr Fly—a fly emphasizing just these features—has proven itself on Alaska's rainbow trout, Arctic char, Dolly Varden, and steelhead. Hank fishes this pattern with an active left hand, imitating both darting and resting behaviors.

POLAR CHUB BUCKTAIL

Hook: *Tiemco 300, sizes 2-6*
Thread: *Black*
Tail: *White polar bear or substitute*
Body: *Tapered floss base coated with lacquer; large oval silver tinsel wound over the wet lacquer*
Wing: *Three layers: from bottom to top—white, olive green, and brown polar bear hair or substitutes*
Cheeks: *Jungle cock (optional)*
Head: *Painted brown op top, pale green underneath*

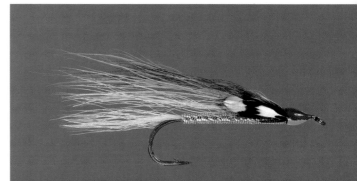

Originated by E. H. (Polly) Rosborough in 1955 as a baitfish imitation, the Polar Chub is an effective pattern for many species of fresh and saltwater gamefish. In Alaska, try this fly in spring or early summer when rainbows and char "fill up" on migrating smolt.

REGGIE MILLER

Hook: *Eagle Claw 1197G, sizes 4-6*
Thread: *Black*
Body: *Silver tinsel chenille*
Wing: *Cream polar bear hair or substitute over which is tied*

black bucktail with Lady Amherst crests on each side
Topping: *Five or six strands of peacock herl*
Cheeks: *Jungle cock (optional)*

This variation on the Sockeye John theme tied by Dan Flanders is effective for rainbow trout and Dolly Varden in the Bristol Bay area. The Reggie Miller was named for a streamside acquaintance who accepted and fished some of Flanders' flies when his own supply was exhausted. Later, he most graciously sent Dan a jungle cock cape.

RON'S DARK CHENILLE SCULPIN

Hook: *Mustad 9672, sizes 2-6*
Thread: *Black*
Tail: *Two mallard feathers, dyed wood duck color*
Body: *Variegated ginger and brown chenille, weighted*
Ribbing: *Oval gold tinsel*
Hackle: *Cree*

Wing: *Two Cree hackles and two furnace hackles*
Underwing: *Fox squirrel tail*
Fins: *Mallard breast feather, dyed wood duck color*
Head: *Size 5/0 variegated ginger and brown chenille; clip top and bottom to make a flat head*

Ron Clauson designed this version of the sculpin with a chenille head rather than the traditional clipped deer hair. This allows the fly to sink faster and deeper. It is most effective when bounced along the bottom, then retrieved across and upstream after it swings around. The fish will usually strike the instant the fly stops in the swing and the retrieve begins.

RON'S TUKABOO SCULPIN

Hook: *Mustad 9672, sizes 2/0-6*
Thread: *Black*
Tail: *Two mallard feathers dyed brown*
Body: *Variegated ginger and brown chenille, weighted*

Ribbing: *Oval gold tinsel*
Wing: *Black and brown marabou tied Matuka style*
Fins: *Teal body feathers dyed brown*
Head: *Dark brown deer body hair, spun and trimmed flat*

This is one of the beautiful patterns tied by Ron Clauson that is very good for large rainbows, Arctic char, and grayling. A good way to fish it is to cast across stream or slightly upstream, let the fly bounce along the bottom, then hold on, particularly as it swings around at the end of the drift.

SALMON FRY

Hook: *Mustad 9575, sizes 8-12*
Thread: *Olive or brown*
Eyes: *Small silver bead chain*

Wing: *Gold Krystal Flash topped by olive or brown bucktail*

This fly is tied upside-down (to reduce snagging) and simply (to facilitate replacement). It is fished on a dead drift interspersed with twitches and mends to enhance the illusion of life, an illusion Hank Pennington performs across Bristol Bay, Kodiak Island, and the Alaska Peninsula. Recently, Hank discovered that large Dolly Varden prefer this pattern over spawn imitations—maybe the Dollies are finally getting tired of eggs.

SILVER BROWN BUCK

Hook: *Tiemco 5263, sizes 4-10*
Thread: *White*
Body: *Flat silver tinsel*

Hackle: *Dark brown*
Wing: *Natural brown bucktail*

This is one of Roderick Haig-Brown's simple, durable and effective patterns for steelhead, Dolly Varden, cutthroat, and rainbow trout. It works best in very clear water.

SOCKEYE FRY

Hook: *Mustad 36620, sizes 10-12*
Threads: *White; red to simulate gills*
Body: *Flat silver or pearlescent tinsel*
Wing: *White bucktail on bottom* *and natural brown bucktail on top, tied Thunder Creek style*
Eyes: *Painted yellow with black pupil*

This variation of Keith Fulsher's Thunder Creek series evolved over many seasons of testing on the Brooks River. Ames Luce of Anchorage showed a more heavily dressed version of the fly to Norval Netsch in 1982. Norval and Dirk Derksen found that a sparse tie was superior in simulating the abundant sockeye fry that flourish in the clear waters of the Brooks and other southwest Alaska salmon rivers. Cast across stream with a floating line and remember to mend the line to allow the fly to move at the same speed as the current. The Sockeye Fry has accounted for many rainbows, Dolly Varden, and grayling.

SOCKEYE JOHN (VARIATION)

Hook: *Eagle Claw 1197G, sizes 4-6*
Thread: *Black*
Tail: *Black bucktail*
Body: *Flat silver tinsel*
Ribbing: *Oval silver tinsel*
Wing: *Cream polar bear hair, or substitute, over which is tied black bucktail with Lady Amherst pheasant crest on each side*

This smolt imitation is especially effective for large rainbows in the Katmai and Iliamna drainages. The originator is said to have been long-time Alaska guide and outdoorsman John Walatka. One widespread version of the pattern is attributed to Kay Mitsuoshi. The variation described here was developed by Dan Flanders at the request of, and from descriptions by, anglers who needed more flies for the next day's fishing at Brooks Camp in Katmai National Park.

S.O.S. (SON OF A SALMON)

Hook: *Eagle Claw 1197G, sizes 1-6*
Thread: *Black*
Tail: *Red hackle fibers and silver mylar tubing, unraveled*
Body: *Silver tinsel chenille*
Throat: *Red hackle fibers*
Wing: *White marabou with one barred grizzly saddle hackle on each side*
Topping: *Peacock herl*
Cheeks: *Jungle cock (optional)*

Developed by Chris Goll as a clearwater smolt and fry imitator, the S.O.S. is used for trophy size rainbow trout in waters where large numbers of sockeye smolt occur. It is most productive when fished just under the surface during the hours of low light between sunset and sunrise.

SPORTSMAN SPECIAL

Hook: *Tiemco 5263, sizes 2-6*
Thread: *Black*
Tail: *Polar bear dyed red, or substitute*
Body: *Orange floss*
Ribbing: *Flat silver tinsel*
Wing: *Black bear hair over which is tied red polar bear hair*
Hackle: *Red*
Cheeks: *Jungle cock (optional)*

The Sportsman's Lodge, located on the west bank of the Kenai River just across from the mouth of the Russian River, sold this streamer to visiting fishermen up through the middle-to-late 1960's. One of the original flies still in the possession of Don Skidmore has jungle cock eyes at the shoulder—a luxury now seldom seen. It was and still is a good pattern for sockeye salmon and a host of other species.

SQUIRREL HAIR SMOLT

Hook: *Mustad 9672, sizes 2-8*
Thread: *White*
Body: *Flat silver tinsel*
Ribbing: *Oval gold tinsel*
Throat: *White calf tail over which is tied red calf tail*
Wing: *Lower one-third is gray squirrel tail; upper two-thirds is fox squirrel tail*
Topping: *Five to ten strands of peacock herl*

Norval Netsch developed this pattern to imitate juvenile salmon that are fed upon by rainbow trout, Dolly Varden and other species in many areas of Alaska. It is also effective for pink, chum, and coho salmon even though they do not feed while in freshwater. This fly has been most effective in very clear water on medium to large rivers. Norval is past president and honorary life member of the Alaska Flyfishers.

SUPERVISOR

Hook: *Mustad 9575, sizes 2-6*
Thread: *Black*
Tail: *Red wool*
Body: *Medium flat silver tinsel*
Ribbing: *Small oval silver tinsel (optional)*
Throat: *White hackle fibers (optional)*

Wing: *White bucktail over which are four light blue saddle hackles*
Topping: *Six or seven strands of peacock herl*
Shoulders: *Pale green saddle hackle*
Cheeks: *Jungle cock (optional)*

This streamer was originated in 1925 by Joseph S. Stickney of Saco, Maine, to simulate fingerling smelt that are important in the diet of brook trout. The Supervisor, named for Stickney's title of Warden Supervisor, is a good fly in Alaska too, because it is a reasonable likeness of area salmon smolts. A modified version, called the Bucktail Supervisor, is tied with a mylar body and green-dyed brown bucktail over the wing. Both are effective for rainbow, Dolly Varden, and grayling in spring and early summer.

UNCLE ROGER

Hook: *Mustad 36717, size 2*
Thread: *Black*
Tail: *White calf tail*
Body: *Rear one-third pale blue angora wool, front two-thirds*

brown yarn, weighted
Ribbing: *Flat gold tinsel*
Wing: *Yellow bucktail over which is tied black bucktail with brown-dyed grizzly hackles on each side*

This is a favorite pattern of a small but growing group of Anchorage fishermen for use in the trophy fish waters on the Alaska Peninsula. It is good for rainbow, salmon, and Dolly Varden, and should be fished dead drift on the bottom.

WINNIPESAUKEE SMELT

Hook: *Partridge CS17, sizes 2-6*
Thread: *Black*
Tail: *Golden pheasant tippet fibers*
Body: *Flat silver tinsel*
Ribbing: *Medium oval silver tinsel*
Throat: *Red hackle fibers*

Wing: *White marabou topped with five or six strands of black ostrich herl*
Shoulders: *Jungle cock body feathers or substitute*

Another excellent smolt imitation named for the big lake in New Hampshire, the "Winni" is most effective in spring or early summer during salmon smolt migrations.

WOOL HEAD SCULPIN

Hook: *Mustad 9672, sizes 2-6*
Thread: *Brown or olive*
Tail: *Brown rabbit fur strip*
Body: *Brown variegated chenille*

Ribbing: *Oval gold tinsel*
Head: *Olive and brown wool trimmed to shape*

Despite the fact that they are among the ugliest creatures of the earth, sculpins are pursued by trout—accordingly, sculpin patterns are common to the streams of Alaska. Dennis McAfee fishes the Wool Head Sculpin with a sinking line and a short leader, working the fly deep along cut banks. He uses the pattern throughout the season, casting to grayling and Dolly Varden as well as to the native rainbow trout.

YELLOW MARABOU

Hook: *Mustad 9672, sizes 4-10*
Thread: *Yellow*
Tail: *Red hackle fibers*
Body: *Silver tinsel chenille*

Throat: *Red calf tail*
Wing: *Yellow marabou*
Topping: *Six strands of peacock herl*

Especially good for rainbows in small- and medium-sized clearwater streams in southcentral Alaska and on the Alaska Peninsula, this fly is usually retrieved with short "bursts" to take advantage of the movement in the marabou wing. Sizes 6 and 8 are generally most effective. Use smaller sizes in shallow water and larger sizes in faster and deeper water. Other popular and effective wing colors are white, black, and brown over white.

Steelhead, Salmon, and Char Flies

ALASKABOU

Hook: *Tiemco 7999, sizes 2-4*
Thread: *Fluorescent red*
Wing: *Fluorescent chartreuse marabou*
Topping: *Several strands of Krystal Flash or Flashabou*
Hackle: *White*

George Cook first fashioned this series of colorful attractor patterns that work great for silver, pink, and chum salmon, especially along the Parks Highway north of Anchorage. Try quartering casts upstream, mending the line until it has straightened out downstream, then use short strips for retrieval. This action often elicits hard strikes from salmon lured to the pulsating marabou.

ALASKA CANDLEFISH

Hook: *Mustad 34007, size 2*
Thread: *Black*
Body: *Flat silver tinsel*
Ribbing: *Oval silver tinsel*
Wing: *Three layers of bucktail: from bottom to top—white, olive, and blue. Four to five strands of red bucktail along each side of wing*

Here's a pattern for king and coho salmon that works well in the salt as well as in the stream. Jim Cariello learned this pattern from the book *Fly Fishing for Pacific Salmon* by Bruce Ferguson, Les Johnson, and Pat Trotter. They give credit for the design to Ernest Schwiebert. Jim says this is his favorite pattern for kings in the Petersburg area, where he fishes stream pools just above estuaries.

ASTRA

Hook: *Mustad 36890, sizes 2-6*
Thread: *Black*
Tip: *Oval silver tinsel*
Body: *Black sparkle yarn*
Ribbing: *Oval silver tinsel*
Hackle: *Heron substitute*
Wing: *Peacock swords*

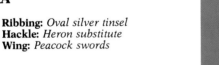

Scott Bryner developed this pattern and has had good success with it for steelhead and rainbows in Harris and Staney creeks on Prince of Wales Island. It seems to be most effective when rivers are high and in the process of clearing.

BAKER BUSTER

Hook: *Mustad 7970, sizes 2-8*
Thread: *Fluorescent orange*
Tail: *White marabou*
Body: *From rear to front: red hackle, unraveled silver mylar tubing, red hackle, unraveled silver mylar tubing, red hackle*

Bill Baker originated this highly visible attractor pattern and has used it in many areas of Alaska for chinook, coho, and sockeye salmon; it is also effective for steelhead and resident rainbow trout, Arctic char, Dolly Varden, and large grayling. Bill has taken many good fish, including a 33-pound king salmon on the "Buster." It is usually fished dead-drift, bouncing along the bottom. A lead wire underbody is optional.

BATTLE CREEK

Hook: *Mustad 9672, sizes 2-8*
Thread: *Orange*
Tail: *White marabou*

Body: *Shell pink chenille*
Hackle: *White palmered to head; two turns of orange at head*

This Pacific salmon pattern was devised by John Spencer of Redding, California. It has been tested in southcentral Alaska streams such as the Talachulitna River, Lake Creek, and the Kenai River where it has taken salmon and resident rainbow trout.

BERING SEA SHRIMP

Hook: *Mustad 9523, sizes 2-6*
Threads: *Black and white*
Body: *Pearlescent mylar tubing*
Antennae: *A few strands of Krystal Flash*
Carapace: *Flame orange over white wool; unravel about one inch of each at bend of hook*
Legs: *White and orange marabou*

mixed
Tail: *Pearlescent mylar tubing unraveled and a few strands of Krystal Flash*
Tying tip: *Shrimp swim "backwards"; parts in this pattern are tied in reverse of the usual order*

If your destination is the Russian or Anchor rivers on the Kenai Peninsula, then this bright fly would be a good choice for sockeye, chinook, and silver salmon. Mike Robinson designed and tested this pattern over several years; he advises that it has outfished all other flies he has used for salmon and steelhead.

BLACK JACK

Hook: *Mustad 36890, sizes 2-6*
Thread: *Black*
Body: *Silver tinsel rope*

Ribbing: *Fluorescent pink saddle hackles; palmered*
Wing: *Fine black bear hair*

Bruce Susinger of Anchorage is a veteran steelhead and salmon fly fisher. He first tried this attractive hairwing pattern on the Anchor River in 1984 and later fished it on the Theodore and upper Kenai rivers. Bruce has taken many steelhead, silver salmon, and a 28-pound king salmon with the Black Jack. This pattern should be fished with a floating line; use twist-on lead approximately 18 inches above the fly to get it down in deeper pools.

BLACK OPTIC

Hook: *Mustad 7970, sizes 2-4*
Thread: *Black*
Body: *Oval gold tinsel*
Wing: *Black bear hair*
Hackle: *Black*
Head: *Split brass bead painted*

black with white eye and black pupil
Tying tip: *Leave ample room for the head; build up a thread base before crimping bead onto hook*

Optic fly patterns were developed for steelhead in the 1930's by northern California fly tier Jim Pray. Kodiak Island fly caster Hank Pennington uses this variation for steelhead and silver salmon on his home island, the Alaska Peninsula, and in the Situk River in southeast Alaska. Hank recommends that optics be fished on a floating line with long leaders, keeping them near the bottom on a dead drift.

BOSS

Hook: *Mustad 36890, sizes 2-8*
Thread: *Black*
Tag: *Oval silver tinsel*
Tail: *Black calf tail*

Body: *Black chenille, weighted*
Ribbing: *Oval silver tinsel*
Hackle: *Fluorescent orange*
Eyes: *Bead chain*

A heavy fly that gets down deep to big fish, the Boss is effective for trout, steelhead, and salmon and is good in fast water.

BUNNY FLY

Hook: *Mustad 9672, sizes 4-8*
Thread: *To match body*
Tail: *End of rabbit strip to be wound as body*

Body: *Rabbit strip (black, ginger, white, yellow, orange, or red); weighted*

Originally designed for bass, this simple pattern has been adopted by legions of fly fishers in Alaska. A gray Bunny Fly was shown to Steve Johnson of Talaview Lodge by a client from the Orange County (California) Fly Fishers in the early 1980's. Steve remembers that the fly outfished every other pattern tried during that week on the lower Talachulitna River. Steve obtained a copy, started tying it in different colors (his favorite is yellow), and shared the Bunny Fly with many flyfishers including Club member Bill Comfort. Bill demonstrated the Bunny Fly to the Alaska Flyfishers at the July, 1985 meeting—it seemed to come into general use shortly thereafter. It can be tied in a wide array of colors and has been found effective for virtually all freshwater sport fish in the state. Fish this fly near the bottom to simulate sculpin (ginger color), decaying salmon flesh (orange and white), or leech (black or brown). Red, orange, yellow, or chartreuse Bunnies are excellent for wild steelhead on Kenai Peninsula, southeast Alaska, Kodiak Island, and Alaska Peninsula streams.

CARLSON COHO

Hook: *Mustad 36890, sizes 1-4*
Thread: *Black*
Tail: *Unraveled silver mylar tubing extending from end of body*
Body: *Silver mylar tubing tied at*

rear with red thread
Hackle: *Hot pink*
Wing: *White bucktail over which is tied pink bucktail*
Topping: *Peacock herl*

Skip Johnson of Anchorage ties this effective red, silver, and king salmon pattern and has good success with it in rivers and saltwater in the Bristol Bay and Kenai Peninsula areas.

COHO (RUSSIAN RIVER)

Hook: *Mustad 36717, size 4*
Thread: *Black*

Wing: *Red over white bucktail (or many other color combinations)*

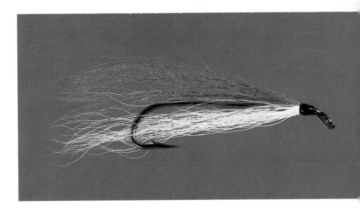

Of the many versions of the "coho" fly, this is probably the most used pattern, particularly for red salmon on the Russian River on the Kenai Peninsula. As its name implies, it will also take coho salmon and other salmonids. The Russian River is designated for "fly fishing only" and the majority of fishermen that line the banks during peak runs tie on one of these flies and use a wide range of rod, reel, and chunks of lead combinations (some even use traditional fly fishing tackle!). It's a good place to catch red salmon and test your tolerance for your fellow man.

COHO (SIMMONS)

Hook: *Mustad 36890, sizes 2-6*
Thread: *Black*
Body: *Mylar piping, wrapped around hook shank*

Wing: *White calf tail over which is tied red calf tail (polar bear is optional wing material)*
Topping: *Peacock herl*

This version of the widely used coho-type streamer is one of the favorites of John Simmons for red and silver salmon and steelhead. It should be fished close to the bottom.

COMET

Hook: *Eagle Claw 1197B, size 4*
Thread: *White*
Tail: *Orange hackle fibers*

Body: *Oval gold tinsel*
Hackle: *Orange and yellow, mixed*
Eyes: *Small brass bead chain*

Quick sinking comets are best used in fast or deep water where it is difficult to fish other patterns along the bottom. These are usually fished dead drift by casting or by drifting in a boat. Comets have been used throughout Alaska for rainbow trout, cutthroat trout, steelhead, Dolly Varden, several species of salmon, and even whitefish. Color variations used in Alaska include red, white, pink, black, yellow, orange, and chartreuse. It can be tied in larger sizes for king salmon.

COPPER AND ORANGE

Hook: *Mustad 36890, sizes 2-4*
Thread: *Orange*
Tail: *Hot orange hackle fibers*
Body: *Medium copper tinsel*

Wing: *Hot orange calf tail*
Throat: *Hot orange hackle fibers*
Hackle: *White*

Phil Driver developed this pattern primarily for Arctic char, although it also works well for large grayling. Char will sometimes just show interest on the first cast, then really take it on the next.

DEAN RIVER LANTERN

Hook: *Mustad 36890, sizes 1/0-8*
Thread: *Black*
Tail: *Black squirrel tail*
Body: *Fluorescent red, orange, chartreuse, yellow, or green Edge*

Bright
Hackle: *Saddle to match body color*
Tying tip: *Body material should overlap itself to expose the edges*

Dr. Art Cohen of San Francisco, California, first used Edge Bright to craft a series of steelhead flies that produced excellent results in the Dean and other rivers in British Columbia. Alaska steelhead are partial to Lanterns too; the "glow" created by the exposed edges of this unique body material really motivates steelhead to strike. The Dean River Lantern is also very effective on sockeye, silver, and king salmon.

EEL RIVER OPTIC

Hook: *Mustad 7970, sizes 2-4*
Thread: *Black*
Body: *Oval silver tinsel*
Wing: *Yellow over red calf tail (or*

bucktail)
Eyes: *Split brass bead painted black with white eye and black or red pupil*

This is another Jim Pray steelhead pattern that has worked well in Alaska. The optics have also been good attractors for silver salmon on Kodiak Island and the Alaska Peninsula.

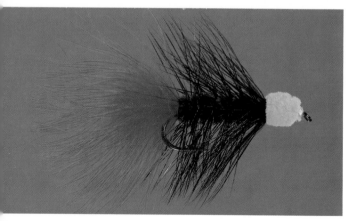

EGG SUCKING LEECH

Hook: *Mustad 9672, sizes 2-4*
Thread: *Black*
Tail: *Purple marabou*
Body: *Purple chenille over lead wire*

Hackle: *Purple saddle; palmered*
Head: *Fluorescent pink or red chenille*

The Egg Sucker may soon replace, if it hasn't already, the Woolly Bugger as Alaska's favorite. This egg/leech hybrid, with the interesting but not factual moniker, was first created by Will Bauer of McBauer's Fly Shop in Anchorage. Since its introduction, the Egg Sucking Leech has been carried by fly casters to the far corners of the state with these results—it catches virtually every sport fish in Alaska's lakes, streams, and oceans. Period!

EGG SUCKING ZONKER

Hook: *Tiemco 5263, sizes 2-8*
Tail: *Unraveled pearl mylar tubing*
Body: *Pearl mylar tubing over lead wire*

Wing: *Blue, purple, or black rabbit fur strip*
Head: *Fluorescent orange or red chenille*

We don't know who first decided to cross a Glo-Bug with a Zonker, but the result was this companion to the Egg Sucking Leech. Wayne Mushrush of Anchorage has fished the Egg Sucking Zonker since 1987 and feels that it is superior to it's "egg-eating" cousin for rainbows, Dolly Varden, and silver salmon in southcentral Alaska rivers. So far as we know, there has been no inbreeding between these two patterns!

EVERGLOW FLY

Hook: *Mustad 3407, sizes 3/0-2*
Thread: *Chartreuse*
Body: *Fluorescent green or yellow*

Everglow tubing over lead wire
Hackle: *Chartreuse*

John Foley of Anchorage developed this attractor pattern for Pacific salmon and steelhead when Everglow material was first introduced. Since 1985 this exceptional fly has accounted for many steelhead and salmon in Alaska. It is usually fished dead drift near the bottom, but try a slow retrieve for silvers.

FALL FAVORITE

Hook: *Tiemco 7999, sizes 2-8*
Thread: *Black*
Body: *Oval silver tinsel*

Hackle: *Hot orange*
Wing: *Orange polar bear hair or substitute*

This popular West Coast pattern is reliable for steelhead, rainbow trout, Dolly Varden, and cutthroats in Alaska. It has produced some outstanding catches of steelhead in the Anchor River.

FIRECRACKER

Hook: *Tiemco 7999, sizes 2/0-4*
Thread: *Fluorescent green*
Tail: *Unraveled silver mylar tubing*
Body: *Silver mylar tubing secured at rear of hook with thread; weighted*

Throat: *Unraveled silver mylar tubing*
Wing: *White FisHair over which is tied chartreuse FisHair*
Topping: *Several strands of Krystal Flash or Flashabou*

Tony Frascarelli saw this pattern in a Thomas & Thomas catalog. He tied some and tested them on salmon during the 1987 and 1988 seasons. The results of his effort were excellent catches of silver, chum, and pink salmon on streams such as the Little Susitna River and Willow Creek. Tony advises that the Firecracker should be cast across or slightly upstream and fished dead drift; most strikes occur as the fly approaches the end of the swing.

FLAME ON COHO

Hook: *Tiemco 7999, sizes 4-10*
Thread: *Orange*
Body: *Gold twist tinsel*

Wing: *Hot pink over yellow over hot pink FisHair*

Ed Atwell of Anchorage fashioned this bright attractor pattern for red salmon. It has duped many sockeyes, as well as silvers and pinks, from the Russian River, Kenai River, and Willow Creek.

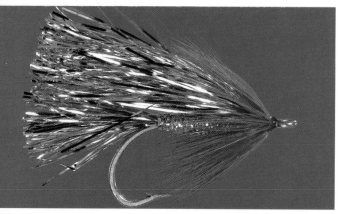

FLASH FLY

Hook: *Mustad 3407, sizes 3/0-2*
Thread: *Red*
Tail: *Silver Flashabou*
Body: *Silver poly flash over lead wire*

Wing: *Fluorescent orange over which is tied silver Flashabou*
Hackle: *Red saddle*

If your target is Pacific salmon, we recommend this deadly attractor. It was originally named the Karluk Flash Fly, after the Kodiak Island river where it was first tested on giant silvers. This pattern has proven effective on many salmon streams throughout the state—it belongs in the fly box of every salmon fisher.

FLESH FLY

Hook: *Mustad 36890, sizes 2-4*
Thread: *Black*
Body: *White marabou twisted and*

wrapped forward; weighted
Wing: *White marabou from body, tied back*

We admit that this pattern won't place first in a beauty contest. No matter. Rainbow trout and Dolly Varden think it looks good—just like the rotting flesh of spawned out salmon that make up a part of their late summer and fall diets. Dennis Wood of Anchorage ties this pattern in a Teeny Nymph style, and he fishes it dead drift with a sinking tip line and weighted leader.

FRANK'S FLY

Hook: *Eagle Claw 1197G, sizes 2-6*
Thread: *Orange*
Body: *Fluorescent orange chenille*

Hackle: *Orange, palmered over body*
Wing: *White calf tail*

Frank Moore of Anchorage developed this variation of the Polar Shrimp. In streams, it is fished on a dead drift along the bottom. When fishing at a lake inlet, Frank usually casts the fly across the current, allows it to sink to the bottom, then retrieves it with erratic jerks. It is particularly effective for king and silver salmon, Dolly Varden, and steelhead in streams on Kodiak Island. Bruce Bowman once observed Frank catch and release 40 steelhead in a day with this pattern.

FLY PATTERNS OF ALASKA

GODAWFUL FLY

Hook: *Mustad 36890, sizes 2-6*
Thread: *Red*
Body: *Vermilion wool yarn or Glo-* *Bug yarn*
Wing: *Pearl Flashabou over cerise marabou over vermilion yarn*

Oregon State University retired fisheries professor, Dr. Carl Bond, designed this productive attractor for Kodiak Island silvers. It should be fished with sufficient split shot to hold it near the bottom, especially when fished in riffles and deep runs.

GOLDEN OLIVE

Hook: *Tiemco 7999, sizes 2-4*
Thread: *Black*
Tail: *Ringneck pheasant tail fibers*
Body: *Gold floss*
Ribbing: *Medium copper tinsel*
Hackle: *White*
Wing: *Olive calf tail over which is tied hot orange calf tail*

Phil Driver uses the Golden Olive for Arctic char and grayling on bright clear days when the water is low on the Wulik River. He employs a sinking line, casts across the river, and lets the fly drift downstream along the bottom. Char usually hit just as the fly swings in the current.

GREEN APPLE NYMPH

Hook: *Mustad 36890, sizes 4-8*
Thread: *Black*
Tail: *Peacock sword*
Body: *Apple green or red yarn; weighted*
Thorax: *Apple green or red yarn*
Wingcase: *Eight to ten strands of peacock herl, ends clipped long for legs, divided and tied back*

Hank Pennington has learned that Kodiak Island sockeye salmon, after a short tenure in fresh water, often bolt at the sight of large, conventional streamers and attractor patterns. He formed this unlikely looking pattern that, when presented in a dead drift technique, resulted in good catches of sockeyes, as well as pink and chum salmon. In salt water, fish it weighted. A variation, the Red Apple Nymph, is tied with a red yarn body and thorax.

GREEN BUTT SKUNK

Hook: *Tiemco 7999, sizes 2-10*
Thread: *Black*
Tail: *Red hackle fibers*
Butt: *Fluorescent green chenille*
Body: *Black chenille*
Hackle: *Black*
Wing: *White polar bear hair or substitute*

Some anglers feel that this version is even more effective than the original Skunk for steelhead and large rainbow trout. The Green Butt Skunk will frequently take fish when the regular Skunk will not.

GREEN EYES

Hook: *Gamakatsu Octopus (Red), sizes 1-6*
Thread: *Cerise*
Wing: *Apple green yarn*

"Keep it simple and sparse" is Hank Pennington's advice for sockeye salmon patterns for Kodiak Island. Hank notes that this may be an "embarassing pattern to carry around, but once you have fished it...you will be an advocate." Use a floating line to fish it very slowly in the salt, or dead drift it near the bottom in rivers.

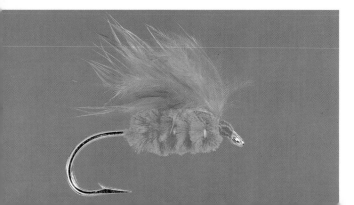

HAIR SKYKOMISH

Hook: *Tiemco 7999, sizes 4-6*
Thread: *Black*
Tail: *Yellow and red calf tail or bucktail*
Body: *Red chenille*

Ribbing: *Flat gold tinsel*
Wing: *Three layers of calf tail or bucktail: from bottom to top—red, yellow, and red*
Throat: *Yellow calf tail or bucktail*

Created by Don Fleming on the bank of Chunilna Creek, simply because he did not have the correct materials to tie a standard Skykomish Sunrise. This pattern is effective in most streams in Alaska for all species of salmon and trout. Don claims that if tied in black and white colors, it catches only hen fish. Some may doubt that tale, but it is true that Fred Babcock's eight-year-old son caught three pink salmon at the mouth of Bird Creek with this pattern when a large number of hardware spin fishermen were either getting skunked or could only snag the fish.

HOT PINK SPARKLER

Hook: *Mustad 7970, sizes 2-4*
Thread: *Black*
Tail: *White polar bear hair (or substitute) and three or four strands of silver mylar*
Body: *Hot pink chenille*

Ribbing: *Medium oval silver tinsel*
Wing: *White polar bear hair topped with five or six strands of silver mylar*
Throat: *White polar bear hair*

Designed and fished by Phil Driver for Arctic char in the Wulik River, it is usually worked along the bottom with a sinking line and relatively short leader.

IRISH SPIRIT

Hook: *Mustad 3407, sizes 1/0-4*
Thread: *Chartreuse*
Tail: *Two green saddle hackles splayed outward, chartreuse Glo-*

Bug yarn, pearl Flashabou
Collar: *Green marabou wound hackle style*
Hackle: *Green saddle*

This Wayne Mushrush creation has deceived many king salmon in Kenai Peninsula streams and estuaries on the east side of Cook Inlet. The tarpon fly style head prevents the wing materials from wrapping around the hook.

JOCK SCOTT (HAIR WING)

Hook: *Tiemco 7999, sizes 2-6*
Tag: *Flat silver tinsel*
Tip: *Yellow floss*
Tail: *Golden pheasant crest, and blended strands of fluorescent red and orange floss*
Butt: *Black ostrich herl*
Body: *Rear half is golden yellow floss, veiled above and below with yellow hackle tips and butted with black ostrich herl; front half is black floss*

Ribbing: *Fine oval silver tinsel over rear half, wider oval silver tinsel over front half*
Throat: *Speckled guinea fowl*
Wing: *Red squirrel tail, over four to five strands each of yellow, red and blue polar bear hair (or substitute), topped with golden pheasant crest*
Shoulders: *Jungle cock eye and a few blue hackle fibers*
Cheeks: *Kingfisher or substitute*

Atlantic salmon fishers the world over know the Jock Scott. This and other traditional Atlantic salmon patterns have a following in Alaska where they have been used to take Pacific salmon and steelhead. This hairwing version employs readily available materials for a slightly sparser tie than the original featherwing.

LITTLE LEO

Hook: *Eagle Claw 1197N, sizes 4-8*
Thread: *Cerise*
Body: *Flame orange chenille*

Wing: *"Marabou" from a blue saddle hackle*

Leo Hammer of Anchorage described this pattern to Hank Pennington as the two discussed steelhead flies on the banks of the Situk River near Yakutat. Leo revealed to Hank that he was color blind, which surely accounts for the "clashing" shades in this fly. Nevertheless, the fly proved to be the best of that and other steelhead trips on the Situk. Ken Fanning of Yakutat Lodge says that the Little Leo is still a hot producer.

LONESOME

Hook: *Mustad 36890, sizes 2-6*
Thread: *Black*
Tail: *Hot pink calf tail*
Body: *Silver oval tinsel*
Wing: *White calf tail*
Throat: *Hot pink calf tail*

Hank Pennington named this silver salmon fly Lonesome because it is most effective very late in the silver salmon run, when he often finds himself all alone on Kodiak Island rivers and lakes. Fish this one very slowly on a sinking tip line, dead drifting it if there is any current.

LONNIE'S KILLER

Hook: *Mustad 79580, sizes 2-6*
Thread: *Black*
Tail: *Silver mylar tubing extending beyond body and unraveled*
Body: *Silver mylar tubing*
Wing: *Three layers of bucktail: from bottom to top—orange, yellow, and orange*
Throat: *White bucktail*

Developed in 1977 by Denton Mays of Anchorage. In streams, the fly is cast upstream and allowed to drift along the bottom. In lakes, it has been most effective by casting to a cruising fish and using a slow retrieve. It is useful for pink, red, silver, and king salmon in many waters in southcentral Alaska and on Kodiak Island.

MAD MANDRILL

Hook: *Mustad 36890, sizes 2-6*
Thread: *White*
Body: *Silver oval tinsel*
Wing: *Purple marabou over red bucktail*
Throat: *Blue bucktail*

If your destination is Kodiak Island, consider taking a supply of this silver salmon pattern designed by Dr. Carl Bond of Corvallis, Oregon. It has produced good catches in the Buskin River, Pasagshak River, and Roselyn's Creek.

MAI-TAI

Hook: *Mustad 9672, size 4*
Thread: *Fluorescent pink*
Tail: *Unraveled silver mylar tubing*
Body: *Silver mylar tubing over lead*
wire
Wing: *Hot pink bucktail topped by purple bucktail*
Throat: *Chartreuse bucktail*

Gary Miller found that this color combination produced excellent catches of reds, pinks, and chums on Kenai Peninsula waters, including the Russian River, Kenai River, Quartz Creek, Ptarmigan Creek, Kasilof River, and Deep Creek. If dressed sparse the Mai-Tai doubles as a good low water pattern.

MARC'S TIDAL STRATEGY

Hook: *Mustad 36890, sizes 2-6*
Thread: *Black*
Body: *Gold mylar piping*
Wing: *Chartreuse bucktail; five strands of silver Flashabou on each side of wing*

First tested on Kenai Peninsula salmon streams, this attractor pattern has taken many silvers and kings. Designer Marc Van Hauwaert has also had good success with it in tidal pools and estuaries on the east side of lower Cook Inlet.

McLEOD UGLY

Hook: *Mustad 9672, sizes 2-6*
Thread: *Black*
Tail: *Red marabou*
Body: *Black chenille*
Hackle: *Grizzly, tied palmer style*
Ribbing: *Fine stainless steel wire cross wrapped over hackle*
Wing: *Black bear hair*

Ken McLeod developed this fly in 1962, and it has since become a respected pattern for steelhead in the Northwest. Although dark patterns are not as popular as bright colored ones with fishermen, this fly will sometimes save the day. It may be tied weighted or unweighted, but either style should be fished along the bottom. The stainless steel wire increases the durability of the hackle.

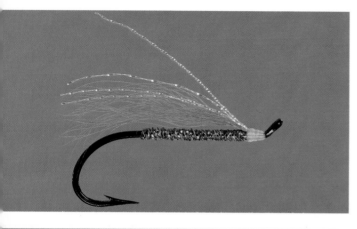

MONTANA BILL

Hook: *Mustad 36890, sizes 2-6*
Thread: *Chartreuse*
Body: *Green tinsel yarn*
Wing: *Four strands of green Krystal Flash over ten to twelve strands of green bucktail*

Montana was the home of the unknown creator of this pattern shown to Bill Polson of Kodiak. Hank Pennington named it and submitted it for publication here because it has been a hot silver salmon attractor on several Kodiak Island streams. Pennington recommends these sparse ties instead of large, bright flies for silvers that have been in the river for more than a day—he says they then "become real connoisseurs of small, slow flies."

NIGHT HAWK

Hook: *Partridge M, size 4*
Thread: *Black*
Tag: *Fine silver oval tinsel*
Tip: *Yellow floss*
Tail: *Golden pheasant crest and blue kingfisher or hackle fibers*
Butt: *Red wool*
Body: *Flat silver tinsel*
Ribbing: *Oval silver tinsel*
Throat: *Black hackle*
Wing: *Black squirrel tail*
Cheeks: *Blue kingfisher or hackle fibers*
Head: *Red*

This classic featherwing Atlantic salmon fly, converted to a hairwing, has fooled many Pacific salmon in Kenai Peninsula streams. It should be fished dead drift by mending the fly line. Silvers can often be enticed to strike this pattern if it is retrieved in short bursts.

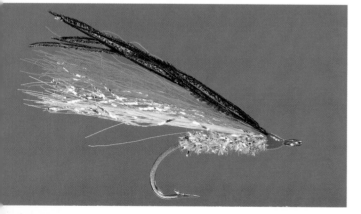

N.W.O. (NORTHWEST OUTFITTERS) STREAMER

Hook: *Mustad 34007, sizes 4/0-2*
Thread: *Flame orange*
Body: *Silver tinsel chenille*
Wing: *White FisHair over which is*
tied unraveled mylar tubing, topped with hot pink FisHair
Topping: *Peacock herl*

This pattern was developed by Chris Goll for sheefish on the Kobuk River. Further experimentation proved it to be very effective for king salmon in fresh and saltwater. Other color variations include blue or green FisHair instead of the hot pink in the wing with a matching color thread.

ORANGE WIGGLE TAIL

Hook: *Mustad 7970, sizes 2-8*
Thread: *Black*
Tail: *Orange marabou*
Body: *Orange chenille*
Ribbing: *Oval silver tinsel*
Hackle: *Unraveled mylar tubing trimmed to hook shank length*

Fishing guide Ron Hyde created this egg/attractor pattern that has become a standby on the Goodnews River and other western Alaska streams. It is effective for rainbows, Dolly Varden, all salmon species, grayling, and anything else that feeds on salmon eggs. Cast it upstream or quartering downstream. When casting upstream, retrieve it in short, quick tugs. An equally effective or even better variation is to tie it with a white marabou tail and pink chenille body. This version is actually the more popular of the two, and is called the White Wiggle Tail.

FLY PATTERNS OF ALASKA

PASAGSHAK

Hook: *Mustad 36890, sizes 2-6*
Thread: *Black*
Tail: *Hot pink calf tail*
Body: *Oval silver tinsel*
Wing: *One-third purple calf tail over two-thirds hot pink calf tail*
Throat: *Purple calf tail*

Purple and pink is a winning combination for late season silvers on Kodiak Island. Inventive Kodiak tier Hank Pennington tested this attractor over several years and found it to be a standout for cohos when they enter lakes. Hank suggests that the Pasagshak should be fished very slowly with a floating line early and late in the day, and with a sinking tip line when the fish hold deep in bright daylight.

PEACOCK BLUE COHO

Hook: *Mustad 36890, sizes 2-4*
Thread: *Black*
Body: *Oval silver tinsel*
Wing: *Peacock blue FisHair or bucktail over white FisHair or bucktail*
Throat: *Peacock blue FisHair or bucktail*

Jim Hemming, a longtime member of the Alaska Flyfishers, enjoys fishing for big silvers on Kodiak Island. Here's a reliable pattern for Kodiak streams that has snookered many fighting cohos during August and September.

PINK FLOOZY

Hook: *Mustad 36890, sizes 2-8*
Thread: *Pink or red*
Body: *Pearl Diamond Braid or Glitter Body; weighted*
Wing: *Fluorescent pink marabou with a few strands of pink or pearl Krystal Flash*

As the name suggests, steelhead and Pacific salmon are often seduced by this gaudily dressed attractor. It has been a very good choice for Situk River steelhead.

POLAR SHRIMP

Hook: *Tiemco 7999, sizes 2-6*
Thread: *Black*
Tail: *Red hackle tips*
Body: *Fluorescent orange chenille*
Hackle: *Orange*
Wing: *White polar bear hair or substitute*

This is a favorite of fly fishers all over Alaska for rainbow trout, Dolly Varden, steelhead, coho, and pink salmon.

PURPLE ANGEL

Hook: *Tiemco 7999, sizes 2-8*
Thread: *Black*
Tail: *Purple hackle fibers*
Butt: *Fluorescent flame chenille*
Body: *Purple chenille*
Ribbing: *Oval silver tinsel*
Wing: *White polar bear hair or bucktail*
Hackle: *Purple*

Steelheader and author Trey Combs lists this pattern in his book *Steelhead Fly Fishing and Flies*. It was developed by Bob Strobel for Washington waters, and we have found it to be a good choice for steelhead on Kenai Peninsula streams.

PURPLE OPTIC

Hook: *Mustad 7970, sizes 2-4*
Thread: *Black*
Tail: *Red calf tail*
Body: *Purple chenille*
Ribbing: *Oval silver tinsel*

Wing: *Black bear or bucktail*
Hackle: *Black*
Head: *Split brass bead painted black with white eye and red or black pupil*

Kodiak Island fly caster Hank Pennington crossed the technology of Jim Pray's optic flies with new perceptions of steelhead color preferences and wound up with this deadly hybrid. It is a very good choice when steelhead or silver salmon are sulking deep and prefer a slow moving fly. Use a floating line and long leaders for fishing the optic series.

PURPLE PERIL

Hook: *Tiemco 7999, sizes 2-6*
Thread: *Black*
Tip: *Silver tinsel*
Tail: *Purple hackle fibers*

Body: *Purple floss*
Ribbing: *Oval silver tinsel*
Hackle: *Purple*
Wing: *Natural brown deer hair*

Here's another Ken McLeod steelhead pattern that has encouraged strikes from many steelhead in Alaska. Alaska has over 360 streams that support wild native steelhead. If your destination is one of these jewels, don't forget to clip a few Purple Peril's in your fly box.

QUEEN BESS

Hook: *Partridge M, sizes 2-6*
Thread: *Black*
Tail: *Gray squirrel tail*

Body: *Silver tinsel*
Wing: *Gray squirrel tail over yellow bucktail*

Trey Combs traced the origin of this 1940's pattern to Peter Schwab of California, who named it after his steelheader companion and wife. Cane rod builder Marty Karstetter of Anchorage has found this old pattern to be "a real sleeper" for silvers. It can be fished dead drift in streams or retrieved in estuaries to imitate bait fish.

RAJAH

Hook: *Partridge M, sizes 4-6*
Thread: *Black*
Tail: *Fluorescent pink bucktail*
Body: *Rear two-thirds silver tinsel; front, fluorescent pink chenille*

ribbed with two turns of pink tinsel (optional)
Wing: *White polar bear or substitute*
Hackle: *Fluorescent pink*

Those few Alaska steelheaders who have tried the Rajah never leave home without it. It is colorful, yet subtle enough for low water conditions, and when tied with a sparse polar bear wing the Rajah is truly a "king" among steelhead patterns. It was first tied in 1967 by Arthur Solomon of Spokane, Washington, according to Trey Combs, who listed this pattern in his book *Steelhead Fly Fishing and Flies*. Marty Karstetter of Anchorage has also found it to be very effective for Dolly Varden and red and silver salmon.

RED HOT

Hook: *Gamakatsu Octopus (Red), sizes 1-6*

Wing: *Red Flashabou*

Puget Sound fishermen sometimes troll a bare red Gamakatsu Octopus hook behind a flasher to catch sockeye salmon virtually year around. Hank Pennington capitalized on this idea, added a bit of Flashabou for the wing, and found that this combination really turned on Kodiak Island salmon. Hank has taken many sockeyes, pinks, and chums on this simple little fly. Fish this pattern slowly on a floating line in salt water, or dead drift it near the bottom in rivers.

RED RASCAL

Hook: *Mustad 36717, size 2*
Thread: *Black*
Tail: *Orange calf tail*
Body: *Orange glow yarn*

Wing: *Yellow polar bear hair over which is tied white polar bear hair*
Throat: *Orange calf tail*

For many years a vast majority of Alaskans thought that the only effective way to catch red salmon was to foul hook them with weighted treble hooks. In 1963, Jim Hemming was at the Russian River and, while assisting a fisherman land a red salmon, was delighted to see it had taken a large bucktail. Jim then experimented with a variety of patterns that led to the development of the Red Rascal. This and the Gray Ghost are Jim's favorites for red salmon.

RED ROCKET

Hook: *Partridge CS2, sizes 4-6*
Thread: *Red*
Tail: *Unraveled silver mylar tubing*
Body: *Silver mylar tubing over lead*

wire
Throat: *Silver Flashabou*
Wing: *Red saddle hackle tips; two on each side*

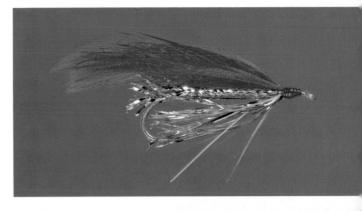

Chuck Ash crafted this pattern on the Branch River after watching a spincaster take a nice rainbow on a Daredevil spoon. Chuck found his attractor to be hot enough to earn this name and now carries the Red Rocket as a standard rainbow and salmon pattern when he fishes the Branch, Koktuli, Chilikadrotna, Mulchatna, Togiak, and Goodnews rivers.

RED THROAT PASSION

Hook: *Mustad 36890, sizes 2-6*
Thread: *Black*
Tail: *Fluorescent green yarn*
Body: *Fluorescent green chenille*

Throat: *Hot pink or red FisHair*
Wing: *Green polar bear hair or bucktail*

Alaska Flyfisher Russell King developed this salmon pattern for the Kenai River and other Kenai Peninsula streams. It has taken all five Pacific salmon since it was first field tested in 1986.

RUSSIAN FLASHER

Hook: *Mustad 36890, sizes 2-6*
Thread: *Black*
Tail: *Fluorescent green marabou*
Body: *Gold Diamond Braid*

Wing: *Fluorescent green marabou over fluorescent green Krystal Flash*

The chartreuse marabou in this Denny Wood creation has attracted plenty of Russian River red salmon. The Russian River has two distinct runs of sockeye salmon—an early migration in mid-June and a second, much larger run about a month later. Denny recommends that his Flasher should be fished dead drift with a sinking tip line, or alternatively with a floating line and enough split shot to carry the fly near the bottom where sockeyes hold during migration to spawning sites.

SILVER FLASH

Hook: *Eagle Claw 1197N, sizes 2-6*
Thread: *White*
Tail: *Pearl Flashabou*

Body: *Silver tinsel chenille*
Wing: *Orange bucktail or FisHair*
Eyes: *Silver bead chain*

Dave Sullivan, a charter member of the Alaska Flyfishers, designed this pattern for silver salmon, but found that it will take pinks, chums, and kings, as well as rainbows, and Dolly Varden. This is a good choice if you intend to fish deep holes or riffle water because the chain eyes quickly move the fly through the water column to the stream bottom.

SILVER HILTON

Hook: *Tiemco 7999, sizes 2-6*
Thread: *Black*
Tail: *Mallard flank feather fibers*
Body: *Black chenille*

Ribbing: *Flat silver tinsel*
Hackle: *Grizzly*
Wing: *Grizzly hackle tips flared outward*

A popular steelhead pattern used throughout the Pacific Northwest and Alaska, the Silver Hilton can also be fished as a juvenile salmon imitation.

SILVER SLIVER

Hook: *Mustad 9672, sizes 4-6*
Thread: *Red*
Tail: *Silver mylar tubing extended beyond end of body and unraveled*

Body: *Silver mylar tubing*
Wing: *Orange bucktail*
Throat: *Yellow bucktail, same length as wing*

Hank Hosking, now living in Gouldsboro, Maine, designed this attractor for Anchor River steelhead. He also used it successfully for rainbows on the Brooks River in Katmai National Monument.

SKYKOMISH SUNRISE

Hook: *Tiemco 7999, sizes 2-6*
Thread: *Black*
Tail: *Red and yellow hackle fibers, mixed*
Body: *Red chenille*

Ribbing: *Flat silver tinsel*
Hackle: *Red and yellow, mixed*
Wing: *White polar bear hair or substitute*

This important steelhead pattern is popular in Alaska for everything from king salmon to grayling. A good variation is the Skykomish Yellow which has a yellow chenille body rather than red.

SKUNK

Hook: *Tiemco 7999, sizes 2-6*
Thread: *Black*
Tail: *Red hackle fibers*
Body: *Black chenille*

Ribbing: *Flat silver tinsel*
Hackle: *Black*
Wing: *White polar bear hair or bucktail*

This is a standard steelhead pattern used thoroughout the Pacific Northwest and Alaska.

SOUTHEAST SHRIMP

Hook: *Partridge CS10, sizes 4-6*
Thread: *Black*
Tag: *Flat silver tinsel*
Tail: *Amherst pheasant crest*
Body: *Silver Diamond Braid over*

which is wrapped orange Sparkle Chenille
Hackle: *Extra wide, soft orange saddle hackle or other heron substitute, palmered*

Jim Cariello ties this beautiful and functional steelhead fly for use on southeast Alaska streams. Jim has had good success with this pattern even when the water temperature was 33 degrees.

38

SPEY DAY

Hook: *Tiemco 7999, sizes 2-6*
Thread: *Black*
Tag: *Oval gold tinsel*
Body: *Three sections of dubbed seal fur—rear one-third light orange, middle third dark orange, front third scarlet*
Ribbing: *Oval gold tinsel*
Hackle: *Heron substitute palmered along rib*
Wing: *Polar bear hair dyed light orange*
Sides: *Barred wood duck one-half length of wing*

During spring this pattern is good for steelhead and rainbows in pools and deeper runs. It has been effective on Prince of Wales Island streams such as the Karta, Klawak, Harris, and Staney. Scott Bryner developed this pattern and prefers Spey-type flies because they provide more movement than most standard patterns.

TANNER'S YARN FLY

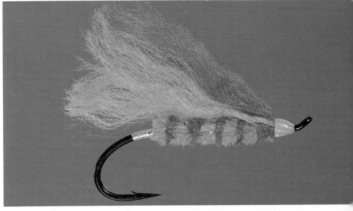

Hook: *Tiemco 7999, sizes 2-4*
Thread: *Fluorescent orange*
Tag: *Flat silver tinsel*
Body: *Orange and red chenille, tied in alternating turns to create a striped body*
Wing: *Orange knitting yarn topped with red knitting yarn*
Tying tip: *Brush yarn out with a shotgun bore brush, then trim square*

E. L. (Don) Tanner began tying this version of the yarn fly in 1963. Although there are now many variations, this one has proved itself over the years for steelhead, rainbows, and all species of salmon, particularly for silvers. This is an easy fly to tie and is very durable.

THOR

Hook: *Tiemco 7999, sizes 2-6*
Thread: *Black*
Tail: *Hot orange hackle fibers*
Body: *Red chenille*
Hackle: *Dark brown*
Wing: *White polar bear hair or substitute*

This is a standard steelhead pattern used throughout the Pacific Northwest and Alaska. It is used for all salmon species, Dolly Varden, and rainbow trout.

TWO MATUKA

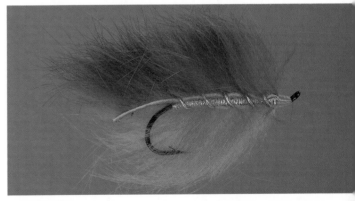

Hook: *Mustad 36890, sizes 1/0-4*
Thread: *Cerise*
Tail: *Extension of purple rabbit fur strip*
Body: *Braided silver tinsel*
Wing: *Purple rabbit fur strip along top of hook shank; cerise rabbit fur strip along bottom of hook shank*
Ribbing: *Braided silver tinsel*
Tying tip: *Tie in under-wing at rear of hook and form body, leaving a six-inch strip of braided tinsel for rib. Tie in over-wing at head and pull under-wing forward. Wet both wings to keep the hair under control; wind the rib forward.*

This purple and cerise blend of rabbit fur has tricked many Kodiak Island king salmon. Most Matuka patterns have just the dorsal wing. Hank Pennington wanted more color contrast, which he achieved by attaching a second fur strip on the bottom of the hook shank. Hank recommends wetting the rabbit fur to keep it under control when winding the rib material.

WILLIE'S SOCKEYE

Hook: *Mustad 9671, size 2*
Thread: *Fluorescent red*
Tail: *Fluorescent orange Glo-Bug yarn topped by unraveled pearl mylar tubing from body*
Body: *Pearl mylar tubing over fluorescent orange Glo-Bug yarn and optional lead wire*
Wing: *Orange over white bucktail*

This brilliant attractor was developed by Willie Morris in 1985 for Kvichak River reds. Since then others have tested the fly on the Kenai Peninsula and found it to be superior for sockeyes and silvers.

Egg and Alevin Imitations

ALEVIN

Hook: *Mustad 9672, sizes 6-10*
Thread: *White*
Tail: *Unraveled pearl mylar tubing*

Body: *Pearl mylar tubing*
Throat: *Red marabou*
Eyes: *Small bead chain*

Young salmon with yolk sacs intact are known as alevins. Spring scouring and erosion sometimes dislodge them from the stream bed and make them available to foraging rainbows, Dolly Varden, and grayling. Wayne Mushrush ties this version of an alevin that features a short tuft of red marabou to simulate the yolk sac. The bead chain eyes carry the Alevin to the stream bottom where predators typically encounter real alevins. Fish this pattern early in the spring before salmon fry emerge from gravel beds.

BABINE SPECIAL

Hook: *Tiemco 7999, sizes 2-10*
Thread: *Fluorescent orange*
Tail: *White polar bear hair or hackle fibers*

Body: *Fluorescent chenille to form two eggs separated by red hackle*
Hackle: *White*

This is one of the most popular egg patterns in Alaska. Fluorescent fire orange is the favorite, but other fluorescent colors, including red and pink, also produce well. A good fly for many Alaska sport fish, it is best used during and after the salmon spawning season, fished along the bottom, dead drift.

BUG-EYED EGG

Hook: *Tiemco 2457, sizes 1/0-4*
Thread: *Red*
Eyes: *Large bead chain*

Tail: *Chartreuse Glo-Bug yarn*
Body: *Fluorescent orange chenille over heavy lead wire*

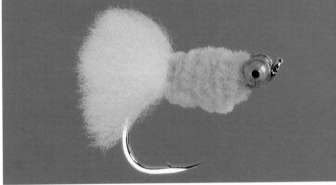

The Bug-Eyed Egg was originated by Dave Sullivan of Anchorage for steelhead in the Anchor River. This pattern sinks well and Dave has had best success with it in the late season, fishing it along the bottom in deep water, dead drift. Dave is a past president of the Alaska Flyfishers.

CLUSTER FLY

Hook: *Mustad 92553, sizes 3/0-1/0*
Thread: *Yellow*

Body: *Fluorescent pink chenille*
Wing: *White marabou*

George Etsell designed this pattern to simulate an egg cluster with milt to be fished while spawning is in progress. It should be used with a fast sinking line drifted along the bottom. George has found it effective for king, silver, and red salmon.

ELDON'S TWO-EGG FLY

Hook: *Tiemco 7999, sizes 2-8*
Thread: *Black*
Tail: *Yellow polar bear hair or substitute*
Body: *Fluorescent orange chenille* *formed into two "eggs" separated by a narrow band of black thread*
Hackle: *White*

As far as we can determine this is the earliest egg pattern originated in Alaska. It was created by E. L. (Don) Tanner for fishing the Katmai area in 1963. It has since proved deadly for rainbow trout, steelhead, Dolly Varden, grayling, and silver and king salmon in both still and moving water throughout Alaska.

FALL DOLLY

Hook: *Mustad 3906, sizes 8-16*
Thread: *Orange*
Tail: *White marabou*
Body: *Back two-thirds is oval silver* *tinsel; front one-third is flame orange chenille*
Wing: *Orange marabou*

Hank Pennington of Kodiak tied this egg variation for sea-run Dolly Varden. However, Hank has found that his Fall Dolly is equally effective for rainbow trout, steelhead, and grayling. This fly should be fished dead drift near the stream bottom.

GLO-BUG

Hook: *Tiemco 2457, sizes 2-10*
Thread: *Orange*
Body: *Two to four strands of flame* *orange Glo-Bug yarn, plus one strand of champagne Glo-Bug yarn, trimmed to egg shape*

Glo-Bugs were developed and are marketed by the Bug Shop of Anderson, California, and are unquestionably among the most deadly patterns ever used for rainbow trout, steelhead, and salmon in Alaska. This pattern is usually fished dead drift as it bounces along the bottom. The standard Glo-Bug is available in over 20 color variations, any of which may be effective at a particular time or place. When wet, the yarn takes on a translucent appearance and "feel" which greatly increases its attractiveness to fish, but at the same time frequently results in fish hooked deep in the throat or gills. Many fly fishers have observed higher mortalities of released fish caught with the Glo-Bug than with other patterns.

ILIAMNA PINKIE

Hook: *Mustad 9174, sizes 6-8*
Thread: *White*
Body: *Flame orange or pink chenille; lead wire optional*

A quick and simple tie that many fly fishers feel is as effective as the Glo-Bug for rainbow trout, Dolly Varden, and grayling. Even the novice tyer will be able to produce a dozen or more of these chenille "eggs" in an hour at the vice. The Iliamna Pinkie can be tied in pink, red, orange, cream, and yellow. Fish the Pinkie with a dead drift technique during the months when salmon are spawning.

KUNZ KING KILLER

Hook: *Tiemco 7999, sizes 3/0-6*
Thread: *Orange*
Tail: *White calftail and unraveled silver mylar tubing*
Body: *Rear portion is orange* *chenille; front portion is orange Glo-Bug yarn tied and trimmed to form an "egg"*
Wing: *White marabou*
Hackle: *Orange*

Mike Kunz originated this pattern for king salmon in the Deshka River in southcentral Alaska. He has since found it to be very effective for king and silver salmon as well as large rainbow trout and Dolly Varden.

MICRO EGG

Hook: *Mustad 9174, sizes 6-8*
Thread: *Black*
Body: *Glo-Bug yarn of desired color*

separated into two "eggs" by black thread

Carl Pearson showed this unadorned pattern to Richard Johnson who has tested it in several southcentral Alaska clear water streams that support spawning salmon. Rich has taken rainbows, dollies, and grayling with the Micro Egg when fished dead drift along the stream substrate.

RON'S KING EGG SPECIAL

Hook: *Mustad 34007, sizes 4/0-1/0*
Thread: *Fire orange*
Tail: *White marabou*
Body: *Butt end is a large egg tied*

with Glo-Bug yarn; the front end is fluorescent orange chenille, weighted

This "magnum" pattern was designed by Ron Clauson to imitate a large cluster of eggs. Ron advises that this fly should be bounced along the bottom through deep holes using extra-fast sinking or lead core fly lines. The King Egg Special has been a favorite for cohos, weighty rainbows, and Kenai River kings, including several that weighed over 50 pounds!

THE PUFF

Hook: *Mustad 9671, sizes 2-10*
Thread: *Black*
Butt: *Fluorescent orange chenille tied to form a salmon egg shape*
Body: *Flat silver mylar*
Wing: *White marabou*
Topping: *Peacock herl*
Throat: *Red marabou*

Skip Johnson originated and uses this pattern for steelhead, Dolly Varden, and rainbow trout. In smaller sizes it is effective for grayling. It is most successful when fished dead drift and deep.

TWO-EGG SPERM FLY

Hook: *Tiemco 7999, sizes 2-8*
Thread: *Fluorescent orange*
Tag: *Flat silver mylar*
Body: *Two "eggs" made with Glo-Bug*

yarn, separated by a short section of flat silver mylar
Wing: *White marabou*

This is a variation of the two egg sperm fly that was originally tied with a chenille body. Some fly fishers prefer to use Glo-Bug yarn because it is brighter, offers a larger selection of colors, and is more durable than chenille. An excellent pattern for all Alaskan salmonids, it is best used during and right after salmon spawning season when fished dead drift along the bottom.

WOODWARD ALEVIN

Hook: *Mustad 3906B, sizes 8-10*
Thread: *Olive*
Eyes: *Small bead chain*
Body: *Braided pearl piping*
Wing: *Two olive hackles topped with a few strands of Krystal*
Flash
Egg sac: *Champagne Glo-Bug yarn with small amounts of red yarn mixed to create the appearance of small blood vessels in yolk*

Paul Woodward designed this especially life-like imitation of an alevin. He field tested it over a 5-year period in clearwater streams on the Kenai Peninsula and Iliamna Lake area. It has proven to be attractive to rainbows, char, and grayling when fished near the bottom of streams during early spring.

Nymphs and Wet Flies

ANDERSON'S PEEKING CADDIS

Hook: *Tiemco 3761, sizes 10-16*
Thread: *Black*
Body: *Gray synthetic dubbing*
Thorax: *Olive synthetic dubbing*
Ribbing: *Flat gold tinsel*
Hackle: *Grouse or partridge*
Head: *Black ostrich herl*

This George Anderson pattern is tied to simulate a caddis larva "peeking" from its case. It can be fished weighted or without lead. Cast upstream allowing the fly to tumble drag-free while mending the fly line. This larval form has produced excellent catches of rainbow trout and Dolly Varden on the Russian River and other Kenai Peninsula clear water streams that support Trichoptera.

BEAVERPELT NYMPH

Hook: *Mustad 9672, sizes 2-12*
Thread: *Black*
Body: *Dubbed beaver fur, thicker toward head*
Hackle: *Ringneck pheasant body feather*

This is a good nymph in a variety of waters but seems to be particularly effective in lakes or slow-moving streams. This pattern will take rainbows, Dolly Varden, and Arctic char and is a favorite of fly fishers seeking large grayling at Ugashik Narrows.

BITCH CREEK

Hook: *Mustad 9672, sizes 4-8*
Thread: *Black*
Tail: *Rubber hackle strands*
Body: *Woven black and orange chenille with the orange on bottom; weighted*
Thorax: *Black chenille*
Hackle: *Brown*
Antennae: *Rubber hackle strands*

The Bitch Creek is a standard nymph used throughout the West. It is a favorite of Bristol Bay guides for big rainbows and grayling.

BLACK BEAR

Hook: *Tiemco 200, sizes 6-18*
Thread: *Black*
Tail: *Black bear guard hair*
Body: *Black bear underfur*
Hackle: *Short beard of black bear guard hairs*
Thorax: *Black bear underfur; tied full*

Alaska Flyfishers member Dave Mitson used black bear hair as the primary material to create this all-purpose, dark-bodied nymph. It proved so successful for southcentral and southeastern Alaska rainbows, grayling, Dolly Varden, and cutthroat trout, that Dave developed several other color variations (see recipes) with brown and polar bear hair. The Black Bear can be tied with or without a weighted body, which permits nymphing from the surface film to the substrate of streams and lakes.

BLACK STONEFLY NYMPH

Hook: *Tiemco 200, sizes 8-12*
Thread: *Black*
Tail: *Black goose biot; divided*
Ribbing: *Fine copper wire*
Body: *Black fur dubbing*

Thorax: *Black fur dubbing with Swiss Straw wing case*
Hackle: *Black, clipped on bottom; gray ostrich herl for gills*

The Black Stonefly Nymph is a modification of Dave Whitlock's Stonefly Nymph No. 1 described in his book *Guide to Aquatic Trout Foods*. This dark pattern imitates the large nymphal form of *Pteronarcella* that appear sporadically in the last half of June in southcentral Alaska streams. These insects are found away from riffles in slower moving water, such as back eddies and side channels, where rainbows find and take them aggressively.

BLUE DESHKA

Hook: *Mustad 9672, sizes 8-10*
Thread: *Black*
Tail: *Red duck quill section*
Butt: *Peacock herl*
Body: *Rear half is silver tinsel with peacock herl joint; front half is dubbed fox squirrel body hair with guard hairs; then aqua-colored ringneck pheasant rump feather palmered over front half*

of body
Hackle: *Aqua-colored ringneck pheasant rump feather*
Wing: *Section of blue mallard quill tied over hackle*
Topping: *Fibers of aqua-colored ringneck pheasant rump feather*
Cheek: *Small blue shoulder feather from teal*

Michael R. Hill of Anchorage developed this pattern, which is effective for rainbow trout, grayling, and salmon. It is a good searching pattern in deep pools and large rivers. It can be fished dead drift or by retrieving it with short twitches.

BRAIDED STONE

Hook: *Tiemco 300, sizes 2-8*
Thread: *Olive*
Tail: *Olive goose biots, divided*
Body: *Two colors of Swannundaze woven flat*
Thorax: *Olive fur dubbing with one*

olive saddle hackle, palmered through thorax with the top clipped
Wingcase: *Swiss Straw or Rafia*
Antennae: *Two olive goose biots, divided*

Developed by Alaska Flyfisher David Ragsdale, this woven-bodied nymph has produced good catches of rainbow trout in Matanuska Valley lakes and southcentral Alaska streams. Dave reports that the Braided Stone should be fished on the bottom of area lakes during summer months.

BREADCRUST

Hook: *Tiemco 3769, sizes 8-14*
Thread: *Black*
Body: *Burnt orange wool or dubbing*

Ribbing: *Brown hackle stem, stripped*
Hackle: *Grizzly*

If you are uncertain which nymph trout or grayling are taking, consider testing the all-purpose Breadcrust. It doubles as a caddis or a mayfly nymph. Importantly, this old standard soft-hackle wet fly can be a good attractor during any season in streams and stillwaters of southcentral Alaska.

BROWN BEAR

Hook: *Tiemco 200, sizes 6-18*
Thread: *Brown*
Tail: *Brown bear guard hair*
Body: *Brown bear underfur*

Thorax: *Brown bear underfur, tied full*
Hackle: *Short beard of brown bear guard hairs*

This is another in the Bear nymph series, designed by Dave Mitson, and used with success throughout southcentral and southeast Alaska (see Black Bear above). The key ingredient in this generic nymph is brown bear hair—a material in ample supply in Alaska. Many trout and grayling have been fooled into taking this impostor for a caddisfly or mayfly nymph. Dave has even had good success fishing this color in estuaries where Dolly Varden forage for cephalopods near the bottom.

BROWN EMERGER

Hook: *Mustad 94845, sizes 12-18*
Thread: *Brown*
Tail: *Brown hackle fibers*
Ribbing: *Fine gold wire*
Body: *Dubbed brown fur*

Hackle: *Brown hackle as a throat*
Wing: *Short sections of mallard primaries*
Thorax: *Brown fur dubbed ahead of hackle and wing*

This is a basic emerger pattern that was once described in the *Orvis News*. Almost any color can be used, but this dressing is effective for rainbows and grayling in Bristol Bay and southcentral Alaska streams. A good way to use this pattern is to dress it with floatant, then cast it across and slightly upstream. Fish it dead drift initially, then let the fly swing around and rise to the surface. Don't be surprised at the strikes you may get using this somewhat unorthodox downstream drag method.

BROWN HACKLE PEACOCK

Hook: *Tiemco 2302, sizes 8-14*
Thread: *Brown*
Body: *Six to eight strands of*

peacock herl
Hackle: *Soft brown hackle of hen, pheasant, grouse, or partridge*

This old standard wet fly is an easy tie. In Alaska, try the Brown Hackle Peacock for rainbows and grayling in any waters where they occur. In lakes, allow the fly to sink before retrieving with short strips of the line; in flowing water, try the Leisenring lift technique.

BURLAP NYMPH

Hook: *Mustad 3906, sizes 10-14*
Thread: *Black*
Body: *Burlap "thread"*
Ribbing: *Black thread*

Hackle: *Soft brown hackle; tied sparse*
Head: *Peacock herl*

This is one of the "Nymphs Plain and Simple" described by Larry Green in the February 1973 issue of *Field and Stream*. Norval Netsch has used this and several variations for grayling throughout Alaska ever since. The thread rib and peacock herl head can be omitted, although the fly looks better to fishermen (not necessarily to the fish) with them, as originally described. Weighted ones are effective when the fish are deep.

BUTCHER

Hook: *Mustad 3906, sizes 8-12*
Thread: *Black*
Tail: *Red duck quill tied to form a "V"*

Body: *Flat silver tinsel*
Hackle: *Black*
Wing: *Black duck quill*

This old English wet fly has been tied in several variations including the Bloody Butcher and Gold Butcher. We have found the Butcher to be particularly effective in dingy water when a bright pattern often will elicit a strike from rainbows and Dolly Varden.

CALIFORNIA COACHMAN

Hook: *Mustad 3906, sizes 10-16*
Thread: *Black*
Tail: *Golden pheasant tippets*
Body: *Peacock herl separated by*

orange floss
Hackle: *Coachman brown*
Wing: *White duck quill*

Fred Babcock discovered the usefulness of this fly one spring in the Copper River Basin near Glennallen. The water was high and muddy, and fish ignored everything Fred presented. After a day and a half of trying one pattern after another, he tied on a California Coachman and began to catch grayling immediately. Arguing with success is difficult, and this fly has been one of his favorites since that day.

CASED CADDIS

Hook: *Tiemco 200, sizes 6-14 Bend the front one-fifth of the hook shank up at a 45-degree angle. Weight the straight portion of the hook with fine lead wire.*
Thread: *Black*
Case: *Two soft hackle feathers trim-*
med to shape
Body: *Pale yellow or cream yarn; one wrap in front of case*
Hackle: *A few dark hackle fibers tied to sweep back below the case*

Caddisflies are perhaps the most important aquatic insect in the diet of rainbows and grayling in most streams and lakes in Alaska, especially southcentral. In his popular book entitled *Caddisflies*, Gary LaFontaine described this pattern which represents a cased form of the caddisfly larva. By altering the color of the body feathers, this fly can simulate either wood-cased or stone-cased caddis larva. Try larger sizes in June and smaller ones in July and August.

DAMSEL NYMPH

Hook: *Tiemco 200, sizes 4-12*
Thread: *Olive*
Tail: *Olive marabou*
Body: *Olive fur dubbing from loop for segmented appearance;*
weighted
Thorax: *One olive filoplume feather with one badger saddle hackle*
Head: *Three to five strands of peacock herl*

Designed by E. H. Armstrong of Seattle and detailed in Randall Kaufmann's book *The Fly Tyers Nymph Manual*, this pattern has gained a considerable following amongst float tubers and other lake fly fishers in Alaska. Damsels and dragons are common in southcentral lakes during July and August, and the tantalizing movement of the marabou and filoplume feathers used in the Damsel Nymph result in lots of strikes from rainbows when this weighted fly is fished with a short stripping action.

DAMSEL NYMPH-PEACOCK

Hook: *Mustad 9671, sizes 4-14*
Thread: *Black*
Tail: *Peacock sword*
Body: *Peacock herl*
Wingcase: *Ringneck pheasant tail fibers*
Thorax: *Light olive dubbing*
Legs: *Black hackle*

This iridescent damsel imitation has received high praise from Alaska Flyfishers club members who have tried it in Matanuska and Susitna Valley lakes. Work this pattern along banks where there is overhanging vegetation or in areas where submergent plants occur. Rainbows are especially aggressive in taking damsel nymphs during summer months.

ELDON'S FRESHWATER SHRIMP

Hook: *Mustad 3906, sizes 10-16*
Thread: *Black*
Tail: *Shellback extended past bend of hook, tied down and trimmed*
Body: *Olive chenille*
Ribbing: *Black thread*
Hackle: *Brown palmered over body*
Shellback: *Gray squirrel tail coated with lacquer*

E. L. (Don) Tanner created this fly in the early 1950's for use in Washington state. Since 1962, it has proven to be effective for rainbow trout and grayling in lakes throughout Alaska.

FILOPLUME LEECH

Hook: *Tiemco 300, sizes 2-8*
Thread: *Rust*
Tail: *Marabou from ringneck pheasant rump feather*
Body: *Filoplumes from ringneck pheasant rump feathers*
Hackle: *One long pheasant rump feather wrapped at two-thirds*
the hook length; wrap a second rump feather just behind hook eye
Tying tip: *In larger sizes many filoplumes will be required for the body; wrap one after the other until desired shape is attained*

This is a slight variation of another E. H. Armstrong (Seattle) pattern that calls for filoplumes. David Ragsdale of the Alaska Flyfishers uses the grayish filoplumes from ringneck pheasant rump feathers, which he has found to be a good color match for some southcentral lake leeches. Dave recommends that the Filoplume Leech should be fished with a fast retrieve to elicit strikes from lake-dwelling rainbows.

GOLD NUGGET

Hook: *Mustad 3906, sizes 8-16*
Thread: *Black*
Tail: *Golden pheasant tippet*
Body: *Orange wool*
Ribbing: *Palmered brown hackle*
Wing: *White calf tail*

Hank Pennington originally designed this nymph for Dolly Varden during their fall spawning migration on Kodiak Island. Hank also found this colorful attractor to be effective for Arctic char, rainbows, and grayling on his home island waters and in streams all along the Alaska Peninsula. He recommends that the Gold Nugget be fished across and downstream. At the end of the swing, allow the fly to swim in the current a few moments before retrieving—you may encourage a trout or char to strike.

GOLD RIBBED HARE'S EAR

Hook: *Mustad 3906, sizes 10-16*
Thread: *Black*
Tail: *Guard hairs from hare's mask*
Ribbing: *Gold wire*
Body: *Dubbed fur from hare's mask*
Wingcase: *Mottled turkey feather over top of thorax*
Thorax: *Dubbed fur including guard hairs from hare's mask*

This versatile and deadly nymph is used in lakes and streams for rainbows, grayling, cutthroat trout, Dolly Varden, and Arctic char. It can be fished dead drift in deep or shallow waters. In streams, allow the fly to swing around and drag in the current. In lakes, use the count-down method to sink the fly to a desired depth, then retrieve it slowly with short jerks.

GRAY HACKLE PEACOCK

Hook: *Mustad 3906, sizes 8-16*
Thread: *Black*
Tag: *Flat silver tinsel*
Body: *Peacock herl*
Hackle: *Grizzly*

This is a simple and popular wet fly for grayling. It is a good stand-by pattern for those times when you're in a lot of fish and they aren't too selective. This saves wear and tear on patterns that are more difficult to tie—a feature that should be attractive to the beginner fly tier. A popular variation is to use brown hackle and a gold tag.

GREEN CADDIS LARVA

Hook: *Mustad 9671 bent to body shape, sizes 10-14*
Thread: *Black*
Body: *Dubbed olive wool, weighted*
Ribbing: *Gold tinsel*
Thorax: *Dubbed dark brown fur*
Throat: *Ringneck pheasant rump feather*

Harry Morrison developed and used this nymph for rainbows, Dolly Varden, and grayling in a wide variety of waters throughout interior and southcentral Alaska. This pattern is most effective when fished dead drift along the bottom in fast water.

HALFBACK

Hook: *Mustad 9672, sizes 2-10*
Thread: *Black*
Tail: *Ringneck pheasant tail fibers*
Wingcase: *Ringneck pheasant tail fibers*
Body: *Peacock herl*
Hackle: *Brown saddle hackle, palmered and clipped on top along rear half of hook*
Tying tip: *The wingcase is an extension of the tail. Secure the wingcase about half-way up the hook shank.*

This all-purpose nymph deserves a clip (or two) in any fly fishers nymph box. We have found that it will take rainbows, cutthroat, dollies, and grayling in lakes and streams throughout southcentral and southeastern Alaska.

HYDE'S UGLY

Hook: *Mustad 36890, sizes 6-10*
Thread: *Black*
Tail: *Wood duck*
Body: *Black chenille*

Ribbing: *Brown hackle palmered over body*
Hackle: *Three dark furnace hackles*
Wing: *Wood duck*

Ron Hyde designed this pattern. It is very effective for grayling, rainbow, Dolly Varden, and Arctic char.

LAKE DRAGON

Hook: *Tiemco 300, size 4*
Thread: *Olive*
Tail: *Olive marabou*
Body: *Olive fur dubbing from loop for segmented appearance; weighted*
Throax: *Olive fur dubbing*
Wingcase: *Mottled turkey feathers;*
burned to shape
Legs: *Two ringneck pheasant rump feathers trimmed on top*
Eyes: *Black plastic bead eyes*
Tying tip: *Use two large weighted nymph forms attached to hook for shape*

This Randall Kaufmann creation has found a "home" on southcentral Alaska lakes where it has proven to be an effective summer pattern for rainbow trout. Rainbows search for dragon nymphs around aquatic plants and debris, so work this weighted fly in and around water lily beds, bulrush, pondweed, and other emergent and submergent plants.

LEADWING COACHMAN

Hook: *Mustad 3906, sizes 10-16*
Thread: *Black*
Tag: *Flat gold tinsel*
Body: *Peacock herl*
Hackle: *Coachman brown*
Wing: *Slate gray duck wing quill*

This is an old standard that could have been named "Old Faithful." It is very effective for many species and is deadly for grayling and rainbow in clear water. This versatile pattern can be fished many ways from very deep to right in the surface film using dead drift, deliberate drag, or retrieved methods.

LENHART'S UNDERWATER BOTTOM SCRATCHER MARK II SPECIAL

Hook: *Mustad 9672, sizes 6-10*
Thread: *Black*
Tag: *Gold embossed tinsel*
Tip: *Black thread*
Tail: *Two mallard wing fibers, one tied on each side of hook*
Body: *Black spun fur, weighted*
Hackle: *Black, trimmed close after completing head*
Legs: *Two mallard wing fibers, one on each side of hook tied slanting to rear at a 45-degree angle*

Bill Lenhart of Anchorage developed this nymph in 1939 for brook and cutthroat trout in Washington, and discovered that it works very well in Alaska for grayling, rainbows, Dolly Varden, and silver salmon. Fish this pattern near the bottom with a slow, hand-twist retrieve.

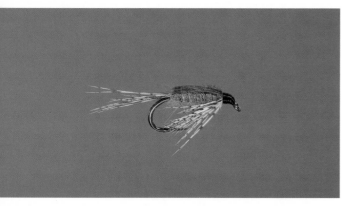

LONGTAIL MARCH BROWN

Hook: *Mustad 3906, sizes 10-16*
Thread: *Black*
Tail: *Mallard breast feather*
Ribbing: *Yellow thread*
Wingcase: *Ringneck pheasant tail*
fibers
Body: *Dubbed rabbit fur*
Hackle: *Partridge on sides and underneath only*

This simple and durable Kaufmann pattern has taken many fine rainbows in southcentral Alaska. Work the fly deep, either by casting and retrieving slowly or drifting it very slowly behind a canoe, float tube, or boat.

MAGGOT

Hook: *Mustad 9671, sizes 12-14*
Thread: *Black*
Body: *Cream poly-dub, weighted*

The Maggot is good for rainbows, grayling, and whitefish in rivers during or just after salmon runs when natural maggots develop on dead salmon washed up along stream banks.

MIDNIGHT SPECIAL

Hook: *Mustad 9671, size 8*
Thread: *Black*
Tail: *Black hackle fibers*

Body: *Black angora yarn*
Hackle: *Black; three or four turns and clipped short*

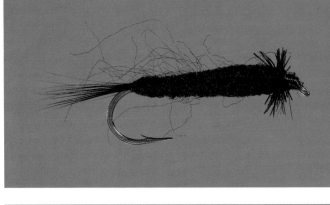

Jim Hemming ties this nymph which has been very effective for large grayling in riffle areas of the upper Ugashik River. It should be fished deep either by tying the fly weighted or by using a sinking line.

MOSQUITO EMERGER

Hook: *Mustad 94840, sizes 14-20*
Thread: *Black*
Tail: *Moose body hair*

Body: *Stripped peacock herl*
Thorax: *Peacock herl*
Wing: *Two grizzly hackle tips*

Due to their abundance and importance as a food source for fish in Alaska, anything that resembles a life stage of the mosquito is very effective. This emerger pattern is excellent for rainbows and grayling in lakes and slow-moving streams. It should be fished in the surface film dead drift giving the line an occasional slight twitch.

MOSQUITO NYMPH

Hook: *Mustad 94840, sizes 14-20*
Thread: *Black*
Tail: *Amherst pheasant tippets*
Body: *Stripped peacock herl on rear*

half; dubbed cream-colored fur on front half
Wing: *Amherst pheasant tippets tied spent style*

Don Skidmore found this pattern in an Anchorage sporting goods store many years ago. He found that it is an excellent pattern for grayling and Dolly Varden in streams and lakes. Fish this nymph near the bottom of streams, allowing the fly to rise closer to the surface as it swings around in the current. Allow the fly to sink, and then retrieve it slowly when fishing in lakes.

MOTH CASE

Hook: *Mustad 3906, sizes 6-8*
Thread: *Black*
Tail: *Black bear*
Body: *Peacock herl tied on full over*

lead wire underbody
Wing: *Black bear hair tied on both sides, the ends cut vertically at mid-body*

After examining the stomachs of rainbow in 1957 on the Green River of Washington state, E. L. (Don) Tanner created this pattern to imitate the dominant contents found. The side wing was added to allow the case to tumble freely with the current. Since 1962, the Moth Case has been used in many parts of Alaska, producing best results on grayling, Dolly Varden, and rainbows.

MUSKRAT NYMPH

Hook: *Mustad 9671, sizes 8-10*
Thread: *Brown*
Tail: *Brown hackle fibers*

Body: *Dubbed muskrat fur*
Hackle: *Brown*

Charles Brooks wrote that a version of this pattern was highly effective for interior Alaska grayling when they were not taking other patterns readily. The Muskrat Nymph has since proved to be an excellent producer for grayling everywhere and will take Dolly Varden, cutthroat, and rainbow trout as well. John Morrison, former president of the Alaska Flyfishers, ties the pattern as described by Migel and Wright in *The Masters of the Nymph,* and uses it in lakes and small streams in the Matanuska-Susitna area. Have weighted and unweighted patterns on hand in order to fish the fly at any depth from surface to bottom.

NIP'S NYMPH

Hook: *Mustad 36890, sizes 2-12*
Thread: *Black*
Tail: *Fox squirrel hair*
Body: *Peacock herl*
Legs: *Badger hackle*

This simple tie was created by Washingtonian Jim Van Tuyl. Brother Dave of Anchorage found it to be suggestive of many aquatic foods in southcentral streams and lakes where he has used Nip's Nymph to take rainbows.

NORVAL'S NYMPH

Hook: *Mustad 9672, sizes 6-14*
Thread: *Cream*
Tail: *Soft brown hackle*
Body: *Dubbed muskrat fur, weighted*
Thorax: *Dubbed red fox fur*
Throat: *Partridge body feather*
Wingcase: *Brown woodchuck hair*

Norval's Nymph is a very good pattern in lakes and slow currents. Let the fly sink to the bottom, then retrieve slowly. Strikes will frequently occur as soon as the fly is lifted. This pattern is especially good in September and late fall at Trapper Joe Lake and other stillwaters in the Cook Inlet area. Fred Babcock of Anchorage originated Norval's Nymph after watching Norval Netsch demonstrate fly tying methods at a seminar sponsored by the Alaska Flyfishers.

OLIVE/BROWN CADDIS LARVA

Hook: *Partridge K2B, sizes 10-12*
Thread: *Black*
Body: *Coarse olive and brown dubb-*
ing mix; weighted
Ribbing: *Gray ostrich herl*

Richard Johnson wanted to imitate caddisfly larvae of the family Hydropsychidae, which are present in many southcentral Alaska streams. He developed this basic tie, which has produced some excellent catches of rainbow trout from riffles where the natural insect lives. Fish this weighted fly dead drift through areas where strong currents have holding water behind rocks, logs, or other debris.

OLIVE SPARKLE PUPA

Hook: *Tiemco 2487, sizes 12-16*
Thread: *Olive*
Ribbing: *Gold wire*
Body: *Olive dubbing with pearl*
mylar tinsel or Flashabou strand
over the top
Legs: *Olive ram's wool*

This Orvis Company pattern is a great caddis pupa imitation in southcentral lakes and streams. Rainbows can't seem to resist the subtle flash created by the single strand of pearl mylar tinsel. The Olive Sparkle Pupa should be fished dead drift in streams. In lakes, try very short twitches of the line to simulate pupa-like movement.

PHEASANT PLUCKER

Hook: *Eagle Claw 1197G, sizes 4-6*
Thread: *Black*
Tail: *Ringneck pheasant tail fibers*
Body: *Ringneck pheasant tail fibers*
Hackle: *Ringneck pheasant tail fibers*
Wing: *Polar bear hair, or substitute*

This pattern by Harry Geron is one version of the many pheasant tail nymph or wet fly patterns that are effective when nothing else seems to work for steelhead or large rainbows. In this respect it can be considered a utility fly. It is particularly useful in large streams and lakes that have a good supply of large caddis.

PHEASANT TAIL NYMPH

Hook: *Mustad 3906, sizes 12-20*
Thread: *Tan*
Tail: *Three short ringneck pheasant tail fibers*
Body: *Ringneck pheasant tail fibers*
Ribbing: *Fine gold wire*
Wingcase: *Ringneck pheasant tail fibers*
Thorax: *Peacock herl*

This nymph is a good choice for grayling and rainbows in interior and southcentral Alaska lakes. It is also very good at the outlets of lakes and in clear water streams. Fish the Pheasant Tail Nymph at or near the surface using a fairly light leader and a floating line.

PICKET PIN

Hook: *Mustad 3906, sizes 8-14*
Thread: *Black*
Tail: *Brown hackle fibers*
Body: *Peacock herl*
Hackle: *Brown, palmered over body*
Wing: *Gray squirrel tail*
Head: *Peacock herl*

This is a good caddis imitation in lakes and streams that produces good results when fished just under the surface using a floating line. This pattern is good for rainbows, and is especially effective for grayling when they are spooked and wary.

POLAR BEAR

Hook: *Tiemco 200, sizes 6-18*
Thread: *White*
Tail: *Polar bear guard hair or white calf tail*
Body: *Polar bear underfur or white synthetic dubbing*
Thorax: *Polar bear underfur or white synthetic dubbing*
Hackle: *Polar bear guard hair or white calf tail*

The Polar Bear is another "generalist" nymph in the bear series designed by Dave Mitson. Dave has taken many rainbows, grayling, Dolly Varden, and cutthroat trout on this color variation. The Polar Bear may represent a variety of aquatic nymphs and larvae.

PROFESSOR

Hook: *Mustad 3906, sizes 8-14*
Thread: *Black*
Tail: *Red hackle fibers*
Body: *Yellow floss*
Ribbing: *Flat gold tinsel*
Hackle: *Brown*
Wing: *Mallard flank feather*

This is an old standard that will take rainbow and cutthroat trout, Dolly Varden, and grayling. Don Fleming, former president of the Alaska Flyfishers, has found the Professor to be particularly effective for rainbows in early spring in lakes throughout southcentral Alaska.

RADER'S KILLER NYMPH

Hook: *Mustad 9672, sizes 10-14*
Thread: *Black*
Tail: *Tips of ostrich herl used for underbody*
Ribbing: *Black thread*
Wingcase: *Mottled turkey quill sec-tion*
Body: *Build to shape with yarn; over-wrap with black, olive, or brown ostrich herl*
Legs: *Small section of ringneck pheasant breast feather*

This life-like nymph was developed by Doug Rader of Anchorage for use around weed beds and lily pads in lakes of southcentral Alaska. It has been a top producer for rainbow trout.

REDASS BUG

Hook: *Tiemco 5210, sizes 4-10*
Thread: *Black*
Tail: *Red yarn*
Body: *Black angora yarn*
Hackle: *Black*

This fly is a very good producer for large grayling and rainbows in the Bristol Bay area. The original was described by Ken Nieland of the Alaska Department of Fish and Game after he was given one of the flies by an unknown fly fisherman on the banks of Lower Talarik Creek in 1972. When asked what it imitated, the response was the descriptive title used above.

RON'S SWANNUNDAZE CADDIS

Hook: *Mustad 94840, sizes 10-16*
Thread: *Black*
Body: *Olive chenille, over lead wire*
Ribbing: *Olive Swannundaze*
Thorax: *Dubbed black fur*

This fly was originated by Ron Clauson of Anchorage to imitate the caddis larvae that are common in many areas of Alaska. This pattern, good for trout and grayling, should be worked along the bottom.

RON'S SWANNUNDAZE DAMSEL

Hook: *Mustad 9672, sizes 6-10*
Thread: *Olive*
Tail: *Two brown hackle tips*
Body: *Olive chenille*
Ribbing: *No. 18 olive Swannundaze*
Wingcase: *Ringneck pheasant tail fibers*
Thorax: *Dark olive dyed rabbit*
Hackle: *Brown*

This damselfly imitation is another original by Ron Clauson, who has made excellent catches of rainbows and grayling in area lakes. It should be allowed to sink near weed beds, and retrieved with slow, short jerks using a sinking tip fly line.

SCUD

Hook: *Mustad 3906, sizes 10-16*
Thread: *White*
Tail: *Ginger hackle fibers*
Body: *Mixed tan and orange rabbit, dubbed*
Shellback: *Strip of clear plastic*
Ribbing: *White thread ribbed over shellback*
Throat: *Ginger hackle*
Antennae: *Ginger hackle*

The *Gammarus* or scud, common in many Alaskan lakes, is a major food item for rainbow and grayling. A good way to fish this imitation is to cast along weed beds, allow the fly to sink, then retrieve it slowly with occasional jerks. Colors may be varied to match the naturals found in different lakes.

SOFT HACKLE ADAMS

Hook: *Mustad 3906, sizes 10-14*
Thread: *Black*
Tail: *Brown and grizzly fibers, mixed*
Body: *Dubbed muskrat fur*
Hackle: *Brown partridge body feather*

Fred Babcock of Anchorage developed this modification after fishing the original Adams as a wet fly. He has had particularly good results with this pattern for grayling in the spring when they are moving from lakes and large rivers into smaller streams to spawn. It is also good later in the season in lakes and streams for rainbows as well as grayling.

STEEL PHEASANT NYMPH

Hook: *Mustad 9672, sizes 4-8*
Thread: *Red*
Tail: *Ringneck pheasant rump feather fibers*
Body: *Alternate red wool, peacock*
Hackle: *Ringneck pheasant rump feather fibers*
Wing: *White bucktail over pheasant tail fibers*

herl, red wool, peacock herl

George Etsell has had exceptionally good luck on Arctic char in the Sagavanirktok and other North Slope streams with this pattern. When cast cross-current, most strikes occur at the end of the drift.

SWANNUNDAZE MAGGOT

Hook: *Mustad 9671 bent to desired body shape, sizes 10-16*
Thread: *White*
Body: *White chenille*
Ribbing: *No. 01 white Swannundaze*
Thorax: *Dubbed white fur*

Ron Clauson ties this imitation of the maggot that is found on salmon carcasses following the spawning season in late summer and fall. During this time, rainbow trout and grayling find this a choice food item. It is most effective when fished by bouncing it along the bottom.

TEENY NYMPH

Hook: *Mustad 3906, sizes 4-14*
Thread: *Black*
Body: *Ringneck pheasant tail fibers*
Hackle: *Ringneck pheasant tail fibers*
Wing: *Ringneck pheasant tail fibers*

Originated by Jim Teeny of Portland, Oregon, the Teeny Nymph Company markets this fly in many sizes, in almost any color combination, and tied several different ways. It is effective for many species including rainbows, grayling, Dolly Varden, and all of the Pacific salmon.

TELLICO NYMPH

Hook: *Mustad 3906, sizes 8-14*
Thread: *Black*
Tail: *Brown hackle fibers*
Wingcase: *Ringneck pheasant tail*
Body: *Pale yellow yarn*
Ribbing: *Peacock herl*
Hackle: *Brown*

fibers

This old standby will catch trout and grayling nearly anywhere. Weighted or unweighted, it is usually fished dead drift. As with many patterns, numerous variations exist, including the use of floss rather than yarn for the body, wild turkey for the wingcase, guinea hackle fibers for the tail and, to add durability, heavy black thread for the rib rather than fragile peacock herl.

UGASHIK SPECIAL

Hook: *Mustad 3906, sizes 4-8*
Thread: *Black*
Body: *Brown angora yarn*
Hackle: *Brown, palmered*

Designed by Jim Hemming to imitate large amphipods that are consumed by trophy grayling on the Ugashik River, this fly can be tied weighted or unweighted. It is best fished dead drift. The body should be fat in the middle with uniform taper forward and aft.

WHITE CADDIS LARVA

Hook: *Partridge K2B, sizes 8-10*
Thread: *Black*
Body: *White floss, overwrapped*
with V-rib
Thorax: *Black hackle, overwrapped*
with black ostrich herl

Designer Jim Cariello has had consistent success in fooling resident cutthroat trout with this larval imitation, which has been tested on many streams in southeast Alaska. It is a durable fly that should be fished near the bottom with a sink tip line, and a relatively short leader since the fly is unweighted.

WOOLLY BUGGER

Hook: *Mustad 9672, sizes 2-6*
Thread: *Black*
Tail: *Black marabou*
Body: *Fluorescent green chenille,*
lead wire under front one-third
Ribbing: *Fine stainless steel wire*
cross-wrapped over hackle
Hackle: *Blue dun, palmered over*
body

This is a slight modification of the pattern described in Vol. 2 of *The Western Trout Fly Tying Manual* by Jack Dennis. The wire greatly increases the life of the hackle and adds some flash. This is an excellent steelhead, Dolly Varden, and rainbow trout producer. Effective color variations used are all black, all brown, and fluorescent orange.

WOOLLY WORM

Hook: *Mustad 9672, sizes 2-14*
Thread: *Black*
Tail: *Red wool*
Body: *Black chenille*
Ribbing: *Flat silver tinsel*
Hackle: *Grizzly, palmered over*
body

The Woolly Worm is one of the most frequently fished flies in Alaska, as it is in the rest of the world. It is good in lakes, streams, and rivers for all species of fish. The color variations used are almost unlimited. Some Alaskans swear an orange body with white hackle is dynamite for rainbows when decomposed pieces of salmon are floating downstream. They call it the "flesh fly."

WYOMING "GIMP"

Hook: *Mustad 94840, sizes 12-14*
Thread: *Green*
Tail: *White hackle fibers*
Body: *Green silk thread*
Hackle: *White, trimmed on top*
Wing: *Trimmed ringneck pheasant*
neck feather tied flat over back

An excellent grayling and rainbow trout pattern throughout Alaska, this pattern was allegedly originated by an unknown Wyoming cowboy who didn't spend all his time punching cows.

ZUG BUG

Hook: *Mustad 3906, sizes 6-12*
Thread: *Black*
Tail: *Peacock herl*
Body: *Peacock herl*
Ribbing: *Flat silver tinsel*
Throat: *Brown hackle fibers*
Wingcase: *Mallard breast feather*

This famous nymph is very effective for rainbows, cutthroat, Dolly Varden, and grayling in a wide range of waters in Alaska.

Dry Flies

ADAMS

Hook: *Tiemco 100, sizes 12-16*
Thread: *Black*
Tail: *Mixed grizzly and brown hackle fibers*

Body: *Dubbed muskrat fur*
Wing: *Grizzly hackle tips*
Hackle: *Mixed grizzly and brown*

An internationally popular pattern, the Adams is a favorite in all types of Alaskan waters where grayling, rainbows, and Dolly Varden are found.

ALASKA GNAT

Hook: *Tiemco 100, sizes 10-18*
Thread: *Black*
Tail: *Black hackle fibers*
Body: *Peacock herl*

Wing: *Teal flank, dark and prominently barred*
Hackle: *Black*

Dave Mitson combined the iridescence of peacock with the subtlety of black hackle that resulted in an exceptionally effective combination for rainbows and grayling. The Alaska Gnat is a good all-season fly that should be tried from ice-out to freeze-up.

ARCTIC SHREW

Hook: *Tiemco 8089, size 2*
Thread: *Black*
Tail: *A few strands of moose mane*

Body: *Natural buff deer back hair, spun and trimmed to shape*

After finding shrews in the stomachs of several large trout, Jim Hemming began tying this variation of the traditional mouse pattern. He has had good success with the Arctic Shrew for rainbows in the Naknek River.

BLACK GNAT

Hook: *Tiemco 100, sizes 10-18*
Thread: *Black*
Tail: *Red hackle fibers*
Body: *Dubbed black fur*

Wing: *Gray mallard wing quill sections*
Hackle: *Black*

The Black Gnat is an old standard that is very effective for grayling and rainbows. This fly can be tied in several variations, including black hackle fiber tail, black calf tail wings and tail.

BLACK SPINNER

Hook: *Tiemco 100, sizes 18-20*
Thread: *Black*
Tail: *Black hackle fibers, split to form a "V"*
Butt: *Black fur dubbed to form a small ball (tail then tied on each side)*
Body: *Stripped peacock herl*
Thorax: *Black fur, dubbed*
Wing: *Black hackle fibers, spent wing style*

This is a good pattern for rainbows and grayling on flat waters after midge hatches. It should be used with a fine leader.

BLUE WINGED OLIVE

Hook: *VMC 9282, sizes 16-18*
Thread: *Black*
Tail: *Moose body hair, split*
Body: *Olive dubbing*
Wing: *Dark blue dun hackle tips or burnt wings, upright and divided*
Hackle: *Dark blue dun tied thorax style; clip "V" on bottom*

The Blue Winged Olive is a good choice for area streams that have hatches of *Baetis*. Fish the tailouts of deep riffles and over shallow runs from late June to late September throughout the southcentral area.

BOMBER

Hook: *Partridge CS5, sizes 4-8*
Thread: *Black*
Tail: *Chartreuse or white calf tail*
Body: *Chartreuse deer body hair, trimmed to shape*
Hackle: *Grizzly or chartreuse saddle hackle, palmered*
Wing: *White calf tail*

In Alaska, the Bomber has been successful in eliciting strikes from silver salmon, steelhead, and resident rainbows. Cast across the stream, and retrieve the fly with short strips, as with a bass popper. The surface movement and noise created by this action often entices big fish to move from feeding or resting lies.

BROWN BIVISIBLE

Hook: *Tiemco 100, sizes 8-16*
Thread: *Black*
Tail: *Brown hackle fibers*
Body: *Brown palmered hackle*
Hackle: *White, tied directly in front of brown palmered hackle body*

This high-floating pattern is used for grayling and rainbows. Other good body colors are black, grizzly, ginger, and white.

CREAM VARIANT

Hook: *Tiemco 100, sizes 16-18*
Thread: *White*
Tail: *Cream hackle fibers, tied long*
Body: *White moose mane*
Hackle: *Cream, tied long*

Fish the Cream Variant during late afternoon and evening when small, light-colored mayflies have a spinner fall. This fly is useful on many southcentral Alaska lakes and streams.

DeLONG LAKE SPECIAL

Hook: *Tiemco 100, sizes 10-16*
Thread: *Brown*
Tail: *White calf tail*
Body: *Olive or tan dubbing*
Ribbing: *Gold wire*

Wing: *White calf tail*
Hackle: *Barred sandy dun, sandy dun, or light ginger; tied parachute style*

John Lewis wanted an extremely visible, high-floating dry fly to attract rainbows in Anchorage area lakes. His DeLong Lake Special has proven to be ideal for several seasons as it simulates a variety of floating insects.

ELK WING CADDIS

Hook: *Tiemco 100, sizes 10-16*
Thread: *Brown*
Tail: *Elk body hair*
Body: *Dubbed olive poly yarn*

Hackle: *Brown, palmered over the body*
Wing: *Elk body hair*

Caddis are common in many Alaska streams, and light hatches may occur throughout the year in open waters. Although not frequent, large hatches sometimes occur; during these events even the notoriously non-selective grayling may become quite finicky. To be successful at these times, the proper size and color of caddis are required. Even when hatches are light or non-existent, the Elk Wing Caddis can be very good for rainbows and grayling. Popular color variations include olive, gray, tan, brown, and light orange.

GANGLE LEGS (CRANE FLY)

Hook: *Tiemco 100, sizes 12-16*
Thread: *Tan*
Body: *Light gray to tan yarn*
Wing: *Grizzly hackle tips, as long as*

body, spent wing style
Hackle: *Grizzly, oversized, parachute style*

The crane fly is found in many areas of Alaska in lakes and slow moving streams. This excellent imitation is effective for rainbows and grayling fished dead drift on flat water.

GRAY WULFF

Hook: *Partridge 01, sizes 10-16*
Thread: *Black*
Tail: *Natural color deer body hair*
Body: *Dubbed muskrat fur*

Wing: *Natural color deer body hair, upright and divided*
Hackle: *Dun*

This dry fly is particularly effective in broken water for rainbows, grayling, and Dolly Varden. Popular color variations are grizzly, black, blond, and brown.

GREEN DRAKE WULFF

Hook: *Partridge L3A, sizes 10-12*
Thread: *Black*
Tail: *Moose body hair, olive elk hair, or dark bucktail*
Body: *Dark olive dubbing*

Wing: *Dark dun or black bucktail or elk hair, upright and divided*
Hackle: *Dark dun, black, or mixed brown and grizzly*

The Green Drake Wulff is an excellent choice for rainbows in the Russian River between the two runs of sockeye salmon. This Wulff pattern simulates the Western Green Drake that appears in small numbers during July.

GRIFFITH'S GNAT

Hook: *Mustad 94840, sizes 18-24*
Thread: *Black*
Body: *Peacock herl*
Hackle: *Grizzly, palmered through body*

The Griffith's Gnat mimics adult midges, and is arguably one of the most effective dry flies available for grayling. This is an excellent choice for stream or lake during any period when midges are hatching. In streams, allow the fly to float free with the current, and on lakes, place casts beneath overhanging shoreline vegetation.

H AND L VARIANT

Hook: *Tiemco 100, sizes 10-16*
Thread: *Black*
Tail: *White calf tail*
Body: *Rear half is stripped peacock herl; front half is regular wound peacock herl*
Wing: *White calf tail, upright and divided*
Hackle: *Brown*

The H and L Variant is an excellent dry fly for rainbows and grayling. The white wings and tail make this a highly visible fly for both the fish and fisherman to follow on the water.

HIGH RIDER

Hook: *Tiemco 100, sizes 8-16*
Thread: *Black*
Tail: *Natural color deer hair*
Body: *Long butt portions of hair used for the tail, wrapped around hook shank*
Ribbing: *Black 2/0 thread wrapped in opposite direction over deer hair body*
Wing: *Natural color deer hair tips*
Hackle: *Two dark-marked variant hackles and one brown hackle*

Kevin Enos designed this pattern for trout and grayling in 1979. It is an excellent floater on fast rivers.

HUMPY

Hook: *Mustad 94836, sizes 10-16*
Thread: *Yellow*
Tail: *Deer body hair*
Body: *Deer body hair pulled over yellow floss underbody*
Wing: *Formed from the tips of the deer hair used to make body; upright and divided*
Hackle: *Grizzly and brown mixed*

The Humpy is an excellent floater for rainbow and grayling in all streams. This fly has proven to be an outstanding attractor pattern. A particularly effective variation is the Royal Humpy, which has white calf tail wings. Other popular color variations of body and thread are orange, black, and fluorescent green.

IMPROVED SOFA PILLOW

Hook: *Mustad 9671, sizes 8-10*
Thread: *Black*
Tail: *Moose hair or fox squirrel tail*
Body: *Orange poly yarn; brown*
hackle palmered and trimmed
Wing: *Fox squirrel tail*
Hackle: *Brown*

This pattern was designed to simulate adult stoneflies. Steve Johnson prefers a wing of squirrel hair in place of the traditional tie employing elk hair or bucktail. The ISP has gained popularity in Alaska where it has taken many rainbows in southcentral and western clear water streams.

IRRESISTIBLE

Hook: *Mustad 94840, sizes 8-16*
Thread: *Black*
Tail: *Deer body hair*
Body: *Spun deer hair, trimmed to*
shape
Wing: *Deer hair, upright and divided*
Hackle: *Brown and grizzly mixed*

This is one of the most popular dry flies in Alaska for rainbows and grayling. It is a very good floater and is particularly effective in fast water. Natural colored deer hair is generally used, but some good variations are tied with black deer hair and hackle or white deer hair and hackle. The Adams Irresistible is tied with grizzly hackle tips for wings rather than with deer hair wings.

KOR-N-POPPER

Hook: *Tiemco 101, sizes 8-16*
Thread: *Red*
Tag: *Yellow floss*
Tail: *Red Krystal Flash, six strands*
Ribbing: *Red Krystal Flash*
Body: *White Evazote strip*
Wing: *White marabou*
Thorax: *Yellow Evazote strip*
Wingcase: *White Evazote sheet, dyed with yellow Pantone marker*
Tying tip: *Do not wrap the foam too tightly or the fly will sink.*

This hot new surface pattern was designed by Keith Goltz to exploit one of Alaska's best kept secrets—the dry fly potential of her trout lakes. Many traditional trout dry flies are heavily hackled, designed to ride moving waters; traditional lake dries are often too large for trout, or too hard-bodied. The Kor-N-Popper is a soft-bodied fly sized for trout, and shaped to move through still waters.

LEWIS LUNKER

Hook: *Tiemco 100, sizes 10-16*
Thread: *Black*
Tail: *White calf tail*
Body: *Black dubbing*
Wing: *White calf tail*
Hackle: *Black*

The Lewis Lunker, designed by John Lewis, is a basic black and white dry fly that has proven to be especially useful for lake dwelling rainbows during the long evenings of an Alaska summer.

McMURRAY BEE

Hook: *Mustad 94840, sizes 10-16*
Thread: *Black*
Body: *Balsa wood in two parts con-nected by monofilament; painted yellow with black stripes*
Hackle: *Black, tied at waist*

The beautiful fireweed plant blossoms attract a diversity of nectar-feeding insects, including bees. Gusts of wind often carry bees and other terrestrial insects from fireweed and other flowering plants to the waters' surface where rainbows and grayling seize them. The McMurray Bee is one of the best terrestrial patterns for Alaska lakes and streams.

MIDGE

Hook: *Mustad 94840, sizes 18-20*
Thread: *Black*
Tail: *Black hackle fibers*
Body: *Dubbed black fur*
Hackle: *Black*

During summer, rainbows in Matanuska Valley and Kenai Peninsula lakes often feed at the surface on very small Diptera. This is one of the few occasions when long, fine leaders and very small dry flies are needed in Alaska. Lake fishermen should always have a few midges along just in case. In addition to black, other effective colors are brown and gray.

MOOSE SERIES

This family of dry flies—Albino Moose, Black Moose, Chocolate Moose, Ginger Moose, and Gray Moose—was developed by Dave Mitson in the mid-1980's. The primary ingredient in all five is moose body hair which, in Alaska, is a readily available and underutilized tying material. The flies are rugged, float well in rough water, and have a life-like segmented body. Any one of the series is a good choice for rainbows and grayling throughout their range in Alaska.

ALBINO MOOSE

Hook: *Tiemco 100, sizes 8-16*
Thread: *Tan*
Tail: *Light brown moose hair*
Body: *Light gray moose hair, two to four strands*
Wing: *Light brown moose hair tied upright and divided*
Hackle: *Cream*
Tying tip: *Tie in body hair by the tips; place a drop of Super Glue on the hook shank, and wrap hair forward*

BLACK MOOSE

Hook: *Tiemco 100, sizes 8-16*
Thread: *Black*
Tail: *Black moose body hair*
Body: *Black moose body hair, two to four strands*
Wing: *Black moose body hair, tied upright and divided*
Hackle: *Black*
Tying tip: *Tie in body hair by the tips; place a drop of Super Glue on the hook shank, and wrap hair forward*

CHOCOLATE MOOSE

Hook: *Tiemco 100, sizes 8-16*
Thread: *Black*
Tail: *Dark brown moose hair*
Body: *Dark brown moose hair, two to four strands*
Wing: *Dark brown moose hair, tied upright and divided*
Hackle: *Coachman brown*
Tying tip: *Tie in body hair by the tips; place a drop of Super Glue on the hook shank, and wrap hair forward*

GINGER MOOSE

Hook: *Tiemco 100, sizes 8-16*
Thread: *Tan*
Tail: *Light brown moose hair*
Body: *Dark brown and light gray moose hair, one to two strands of each*
Wing: *Light brown moose hair, tied upright and divided*
Hackle: *Barred ginger*
Tying Tip: *Tie in body hair by the tips; place a drop of Super Glue on the hook shank, and wrap hair forward*

GRAY MOOSE

Hook: *Tiemco 100, sizes 8-16*
Thread: *Black*
Tail: *Dark brown moose hair*
Body: *Mix of dark brown and light gray moose hair to simulate segmented "mosquito" body*
Wing: *Dark brown moose hair, tied upright and divided*
Hackle: *Dun grizzly*
Tying tip: *Tie in body hair by the tips; place a drop of Super Glue on the hook shank, and wrap hair forward*

MOSQUITO

Hook: *Mustad 94842, sizes 10-18*
Thread: *Black*
Tail: *Grizzly hackle fibers*
Body: *Stripped grizzly hackle stem*
Wing: *Grizzly hackle tips*
Hackle: *Grizzly*

The live mosquito is often called the Alaska State Bird, and a fly pattern imitating it accurately must be tied on at least a 5/0 hook! However, a size 10 is usually large enough and smaller sizes are frequently better. Effective for grayling and trout in all clear streams, this pattern has many variations, including bodies made of alternating dark and light moose mane hairs and stripped peacock herl.

MOUSERAT

Hook: *Tiemco 8089, size 2*
Thread: *Black*
Weedguard: *Monofilament, optional*
Tail: *Brown chamois leather, thin strip*
Body: *Deer body hair, trimmed to shape*

Red-backed voles and lemming populations are cyclic. In years when their populations peak, stepping on them may be difficult to avoid as you walk stream banks in southwestern, western, and northern Alaska. When swimming, these small rodents make easy targets for rainbows, char, and big grayling. The Mouserat is usually cast along stream banks and fished with motion to stimulate strikes. It can be tied in various dark body colors and with optional whiskers and ears.

PIN-HEAD MUDDLER

Hook: *Partridge L3A, sizes 10-14*
Thread: *Black*
Tail: *Hen pheasant quill*
Body: *Flat gold tinsel; coat with cement or clear nail polish*
Wing: *Hen pheasant quill*
Collar: *Deer body hair tips*
Head: *Deer body hair, spun and clipped to shape*

This variation of the Gapen Muddler Minnow is an excellent pattern for lakes and is exceptional in streams, where rainbow and grayling probably take them for salmon fry and smolt. A wet fly version is tied with a black marabou wing and a dubbed rabbit fur collar/head.

RENEGADE

Hook: *Tiemco 100, sizes 10-16*
Thread: *Black*
Tag: *Flat gold tinsel*
Body: *Peacock herl*
Hackle: *Rear hackle brown, front hackle white*

The Renegade is used in a variety of waters for rainbows, grayling, and whitefish. Although it is usually fished as a dry fly, it is equally effective when allowed to sink and fished as a wet fly. It can even be fished by quartering upstream or across stream, letting the fly drift, initially drag-free, allowing it to sink slightly on the swing, then letting it drag in the current.

RON'S BLACK HAIR SPECIAL

Hook: *Tiemco 100, sizes 10-18*
Thread: *Black*
Tail: *Black calf tail*
Body: *Rear half red floss, front half black fur dubbing*
Wing: *Black calf tail, upright and divided*
Hackle: *Black*

This Western type hair wing fly, originated by Ron Clauson, is a good producer for rainbow trout and grayling, and floats well in fast waters.

RON'S HAIR WING MOSQUITO

Hook: *Tiemco 100, sizes 10-18*
Thread: *Black*
Tail: *Gray squirrel tail*
Body: *Black floss*
Ribbing: *White thread, ribbed very close*
Wing: *Gray squirrel tail, tied upright and divided*
Hackle: *Grizzly or Cree*

Originated in 1977 by Ron Clauson to imitate the very common Alaskan mosquito, this fly should be fished dead drift with an occasional twitch. For the few times Alaskan fish are surface feeding, this is an excellent producer and is best used for grayling as they are avid top water feeders. It is also an excellent fly for Dolly Varden and rainbows.

ROYAL WULFF

Hook: *Mustad 94840, sizes 6-16*
Thread: *Black*
Tail: *Brown bucktail or elk*
Body: *Peacock herl with a red floss center band*
Wing: *Brown bucktail, upright and divided*
Hackle: *Coachman brown*

In smaller sizes the Royal Wulff is good for grayling, Dolly Varden, and small rainbow; in larger sizes, it attracts big rainbow and Arctic char. It is usually fished using a drag-free drift, but at times this pattern is highly effective when held back to cause drag, creating a wake. This approach is often effective for Arctic char when they are holding in runs that are four feet or less in depth.

WOOLY MOOSE

Hook: *Tiemco 100, sizes 10-18*
Thread: *Black*
Tail: *Medium brown and medium dun hackle fibers, equal portions*
Body: *Moose underfur or gray/brown synthetic dubbing*
Wing: *Finely barred mallard flank feather*
Hackle: *Medium brown and medium dun*

This Dave Mitson creation has been tested extensively on Kenai Peninsula, Susitna Valley, and Matanuska Valley streams and lakes. The lifelike color combination of brown, black, and dun represent several variations of adult caddis, but trout and grayling may take smaller sized Wooly Moose as a mayfly.

FLY PATTERNS OF ALASKA

Saltwater Flies

BABY NEEDLEFISH

Hook: *Mustad 9672, sizes 2-6*
Thread: *White*
Body: *White thread*
Wing: *Cream or brown dry hackle*
Topping: *Pearl Krystal Flash*

Cheeks: *Imitation jungle cock eye*
Tying tip: *The wing and topping, from eye to bend, should be secured to the hook shank with Super Glue.*

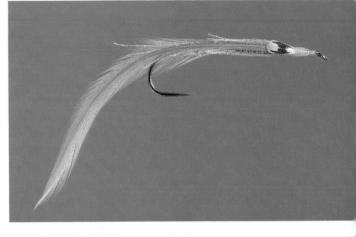

Here is a durable, simple to tie likeness of an important food item in the diet of Pacific salmon, Dolly Varden, and sea-run cutthroat trout. Richard DeLorenzo of Juneau designed this fly to represent the needlefish that are so common in southeast Alaska estuaries. Richard has taken all five species of Pacific salmon, Dollies, and cutthroat on his Baby Needlefish.

ELDON'S TWISTED COHO

Hook: *Gamakatsu Long Shanked Octopus, sizes 2/0-1/0*
Thread: *Black*
Tail: *Unraveled silver mylar tubing*
Body: *Silver mylar tubing over lead*

wire; body formed into a twist, then lacquered
Wing: *White polar bear hair over which is tied blue bucktail*

This is an effective saltwater fly, especially for silver salmon and Dolly Varden. E. L. (Don) Tanner developed this pattern for use in the Seward and Homer areas. Due to the twist in the body, a swivel must be used to prevent line twist.

EMERALD MARY

Hook: *Mustad 92615, sizes 4/0-2*
Thread: *Green*
Tail: *Unraveled pearl mylar tubing*
Body: *Fluorescent chartreuse yarn covered by pearl mylar tubing*
Wing: *Emerald green FisHair topped by pearl Flashabou*
Hackle: *Blue-green marabou*
Collar: *Unraveled pearl mylar tubing*

Tying tip: *Cut an inch long section of pearl tubing for the collar and unravel the strands for one-half the length. Slip the tubing over the head and secure with three turns of thread. The other half is then unraveled, folded back over the first half, and secured with thread.*

Homer resident Bob Moss wanted a coho pattern for lower Kenai Peninsula and Kodiak Island area bays and estuaries. He has had excellent results with this brilliant green attractor during August and September, when cohos school in marine waters before entering rivers to spawn. Bob has since discovered that when tied in smaller sizes and dressed more sparsely, the Emerald Mary is a good choice for cohos and kings in freshwater.

FLAT TARPON

Hook: *Mustad 3407, sizes 5/0-3/0*
Thread: *White*
Weed guard: *Thirty or forty pound test mono secured at hook bend and head with tying thread and epoxy*
Tail: *Eight white saddle hackles*

about four inches in length topped by white Everglo synthetic hair
Hackle: *Four long-fibered saddles on rear one-third of hook*
Head: *White thread, tapered and coated with epoxy*

Few anglers have taken or even attempted to catch halibut using conventional fly fishing gear. Kodiak resident Hank Pennington has landed many halibut, the largest 90 pounds, using 10 to 12 weight rods, sinking lines, and his Flat Tarpon fly. The inspiration for this pattern, as the name implies, came from a style that originated with tarpon flies. The primary and essential difference is the addition of a weed guard, which protects the fly from entanglement when fished on the ocean bottom where halibut live. Hank recommends that this and other halibut patterns should be stripped very sharply at odd intervals; strikes usually come as the fly is settling back to the bottom. Set the hook with a combined hard strip and rod lift, and be ready for some arm-aching work!

HALIBUT GHOST

Hook: *Mustad 3407, sizes 5/0-1/0*
Thread: *White*
Weed guard: *Thirty or forty pound test mono secured at hook bend and head with tying thread and epoxy*
Tail: *White bucktail*

Body: *Silver mylar tubing wrapped as tinsel (optional)*
Wing: *White Everglo synthetic hair over white bucktail*
Head: *White thread coated with epoxy*

This pattern, a variation of Lefty's Deceiver, is fished by Hank Pennington in deep salt water when halibut want a "large bite of food." It is a durable pattern, resistant to fouling on bottom obstructions because of the heavy weed guard. Hank has found that this large pattern will eliminate the frustration of unwanted hookups with smaller rockfish and cod. Fish it on the bottom with long strips followed by inactivity of three to five seconds. Hank advises that color variations are only useful in depths of less than 30 feet. Try a wing of green, red, or orange bucktail when halibut move into shallower waters in August.

HANK'S PINK SPECIAL

Hook: *Mustad 36890, sizes 4-14*
Thread: *Black*
Body: *Green tinsel yarn (Glitter Body)*

Hackle: *Green*
Wing: *Cerise bucktail or calf tail*

Pink salmon in the salt are a most underrated sportfish; they strike hard, fight aggressively, and are clearly an excellent challenge for fly fishers. This Pennington original has been extensively tested on Kodiak Island and Alaska Peninsula marine waters. The results have been many, many pinks landed and hours upon hours of excitement. Fish Hank's Pink Special very slowly with a floating line.

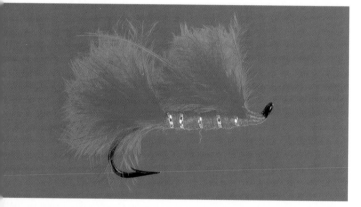

HUMPY HOOKER

Hook: *Mustad 36890, sizes 6-14*
Thread: *Hot pink*
Tag: *Oval silver tinsel*
Tail: *Hot pink or lavender marabou*

Body: *Hot pink yarn*
Ribbing: *Oval silver tinsel*
Wing: *Hot pink or lavender marabou*

In late July and early August pink salmon congregate near river mouths where they mill around on tide flats before entering freshwater. Their ocean diet is primarily plankton, which is what Hank Pennington has attempted to simulate with the Humpy Hooker. Fish this pattern very slowly, moving it just fast enough to keep it from hanging on barnacles and mussels in the tidal flats. Flooding tides are the best times to fish for humpies in the estuaries of Kodiak Island and the Alaska Peninsula.

KALSIN CRAZY CHARLIE

Hook: *Eagle Claw 1197N, bent up 20 degrees just behind eye, sizes 8-12*
Thread: *White*

Eyes: *Silver bead chain*
Body: *Back half—oval silver tinsel; front half—pink floss or wool*
Wing: *Pink over white calf tail*

Hank Pennington decided to try a "Charlie" on his home waters of Kodiak Island after having had success with these flies on Florida bonefish. This variation proved to be especially attractive to pink and chum salmon on the tidal flats of Kalsin Bay and other areas around Kodiak Island and the Alaska Peninsula. Use a short leader and floating line with short stripping action, which will cause the fly to rise and fall in front of cruising salmon. Because it rides with the hook point up, this pattern is a tremendous advantage when fishing around barnacles and mussel beds.

KODIAK CRAZY CHARLIE

Hook: *Eagle Claw 1197N, bent up 20 degrees just behind eye, sizes 8-12*
Thread: *White*

Eyes: *Silver bead chain*
Body: *Back half—oval silver tinsel; front half—green wool*
Wing: *White calf tail*

This cousin of the Kalsin Crazy Charlie is a good choice for pink salmon when they are holding in tidal flats around Kodiak and other marine waters. This quick sinking pattern was designed by saltwater fly fisher Hank Pennington, who likes to use it for sight fishing to cruising humpies.

LAMBUTH CANDLE FISH (COHO FLY)

Hook: *Mustad 34007, sizes 3/0-1/0*
Thread: *Black*
Tail: *One-half inch to one inch extension of body mylar piping, unraveled*
Body: *Silver mylar piping*
Wing: *Three layers of dyed polar*

bear hair: bottom to top—white, carmine, and French blue
Topping: *Four strands of peacock sword*
Head: *Build up thread, then paint a white eye with a black pupil and orange iris*

The late Letcher Lambuth developed this pattern by comparing different color combinations with live candle fish in his home aquarium. Letcher's nephew, Joe Homes, allowed his fishing partner, George Etsell, to copy this pattern from the collection of flies Homes inherited from Lambuth. George has had great success using this pattern for coho salmon on Kodiak Island's Pasagshak River below Lake Rose Tead using a WF8F line with a 12-foot leader. With chest waders and Polaroid glasses, he moves to where he can see the cruising cohos. He then casts in front of the fish and retrieves with short pulls, separated by a pause to simulate darting candle fish. George has also used this pattern for king salmon in lower Cook Inlet, below Deep Creek. There are many variations to the original coho patterns. One, called the Lambuth Herring Coho Fly, is tied with a three-layered wing of pale green, gun metal gray, and a green-blue mix of polar bear hair. Other combinations include yellow over white, red over white, etc., with different color heads (tying thread). The light of the day, weather, and water conditions require trying different color combinations. Don't be afraid to experiment.

MARMOT BAY SQUID

Hook: *Mustad 3407, sizes 2-8*
Thread: *White*
Eyes: *Silver bead chain*
Tail: *White marabou with a few*

strands of pink calf tail
Hackle: *White*
Body: *White chenille*

This simple tie has proven effective for pink and chum salmon around Kodiak Island. Hank Pennington developed the Marmot Bay Squid for deeper nearshore areas and incoming tides. He uses a floating line and retrieves it with erratic strips and frequent short pauses to permit the fly to sink.

MYRTLE MITE

Hook: *Mustad 36890, sizes 10-14*
Thread: *Black*
Tag: *Oval silver tinsel*

Body: *Apple green yarn*
Hackle: *Pink, tied sparse*

The Myrtle Mite is a good choice for pink salmon when days are overcast or when fishing late in the day. Designer Hank Pennington recommends that this "plankton-type" pattern works best when fished slowly on an incoming tide.

OLDS BEACH AMPHIPOD

Hook: *Eagle Claw 1197N, bent 20 degrees at middle, sizes 6-10*
Thread: *Olive*
Body: *Olive dubbing picked out to form legs*

Ribbing: *Black or olive thread*
Throat: *A few pink hackle fibers*
Antennae: *Wood duck flank feather fibers*

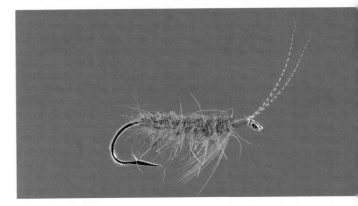

Sea-run Dolly Varden feed on amphipods in the spring and early summer, sometimes taking them in very calm water along steep ocean beaches. This Hank Pennington fly is a good choice for Dollies when they are cruising just under the surface and refuse baitfish immitations.

PACIFIC HERRING

Hook: *Gamakatsu Octopus, sizes 4/0-1/0*
Thread: *White*
Eyes: *6 mm glass, painted with blue lacquer*
Tail: *White rabbit fur strip*
Wing: *Four blue saddle hackles in—*

side two lime green saddle hackles over white rabbit fur strip
Topping: *Peacock herl over pearl mylar*
Throat: *Blue marabou*
Head: *Painted with blue lacquer*

Wayne Mushrush created this big saltwater pattern for Cook Inlet chinook and coho salmon. You'll need a 10 weight rod to move this fly, a short (3-5 feet) leader, and a lead core line for fish that cruise remarkably close to beaches near river mouths. Wayne uses chest waders for casting in the cold surf of Cook Inlet, where he has connected with some heart-stopping kings.

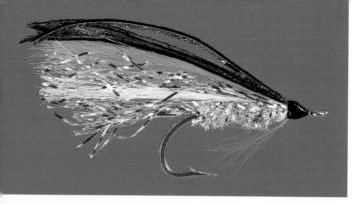

RON'S HERRING

Hook: *Mustad 34007, sizes 4/0-1/0*
Thread: *Black*
Tail: *Silver mylar tubing, unraveled*
Body: *Silver tinsel chenille*
Wing: *Five layers: from bottom to top—white FisHair, unraveled*
silver mylar tubing, lime green FisHair, gray FisHair, and blue FisHair
Topping: *Peacock herl*
Throat: *Red hackle fibers*

This pattern was originated by Ron Clauson for silver and king salmon in saltwater. It is fished at the mouths of rivers or along kelp beds. It should be retrieved to simulate an injured herring, and can be trolled.

ROSELYN'S SAND LANCE

Hook: *Gamakatsu Short Shanked Octopus, sizes 2/0-1/0*
Thread: *Brown*
Body: *Gold mylar piping*
Wing: *Three sparse layers: bottom*
to top—white polar bear hair, red polar bear hair, black bear hair
Throat: *White polar bear hair*
Cheeks: *Jungle cock or substitute*

This version of the sand lance was developed by Hank Pennington and was named after Roselyn Creek near his home at Kodiak. It has proven very effective for silver salmon in the bay into which Roselyn feeds, and in many other bays around Kodiak Island. Hank ties it in a single-hook version for casting when the silvers are really concentrated on a school of sand lance, and in a long, tandem-hook version for trolling. The tandem hooks are linked with a double 15-pound test monofilament line. The tandem-hook fly can be cast, but at considerable risk to the caster!

SALMON TREAT

Hook: *Tiemco 7999, sizes 2/0-6*
Thread: *Black*
Tail: *About one inch extension of the silver mylar tubing used for body, unraveled*
Body: *Silver mylar tubing*
Hackle: *White and hot orange, three*
turns tied in together
Wing: *Three layers of FisHair bottom to top—white, green, and purple*
Topping: *15-20 strands of peacock herl*

Errol Champion, past President of the Federation of Flyfishers, developed this pattern for saltwater salmon fishing near his home at Juneau in southeast Alaska. Errol likes to go to his favorite areas in a larger boat, then fish from a small skiff, casting around kelp beds using a No. 8 or 9 shooting head HI-D line and a 9-foot fly rod. He retrieves the fly with an erratic motion, fishing at a depth of 3 to 10 feet. It is essential to make this fly as durable as possible by tying in all materials securely, using a whip finish and applying several coats of lacquer to the head. Errol uses other color combinations including white-orange-red and white-yellow-lime green.

SALMON TROLLING FLY

Hook: *Mustad 3407, sizes 3/0-1/0*
Thread: *White or black*
Stinger loop: *20 pound mono*
Wing: *From bottom to top—pearl Flashabou, white bucktail, red bucktail, blue bucktail, blue Flashabou*
Eyes: *Painted white with black pupil*
Tying tip: *To tie in a stinger loop,*
start the thread near the bend of the hook. Adjust a piece of doubled 20 pound mono to length, and wrap the thread forward about one-half inch. Then, pull the butts of the mono back and wrap over them back toward the hook bend. Whip finish the thread, and epoxy before attaching the wing.

Salmon trolling patterns have been in use in the Pacific Northwest for many years, but few fly fishers have experimented with them in Alaska. Kodiak resident Hank Pennington ties this version for silver salmon. He uses 8 to 10 weight rods for moving this heavy pattern with short strips of the line as it is trolled behind a boat under power.

SEA-DUCER

Hook: *Mustad 3407, sizes 2/0-1*
Thread: *Black*
Eyes: *Silver bead chain (optional)*
Tail: *Red saddle hackles inside*
yellow saddle hackles
Body: *Palmered red saddle hackle*
Collar: *Yellow saddle hackle*

Several species of rockfish occur in the nearshore waters of southcentral and southeastern Alaska. They are seldom pursued by saltwater fly fishers, although they offer an excellent challenge and are considered respectable fighters. The Sea-Ducer is a Homer Rhode, Jr. pattern that was tied for tarpon and other saltwater species, but it works great for colorful rockfish when fished with a sinking line around shallow reefs and submerged rockpiles.

Top Patterns For Alaska's Sportfish

Trying to decide which of the 251 patterns we have presented in this book to take on your first trip to Alaska may prove to be a real dilema. All of these flies have been tested, some more than others, and they all take fish. Those of us who live and fish in The Great Land often are asked to catalog our personal favorites for a visiting angler. As is the case for most other waters everywhere, the best patterns for Alaska streams, lakes, and oceans vary with seasons, water conditions, hatches, and other factors.

The following favorite flies for fourteen of Alaska's most sought after sport fish are based on interviews with local fly shop personnel, top Alaska guides, and considerable debate and discussion amongst members of the book committee for this revised edition of *Fly Patterns of Alaska*. We acknowledge, of course, that these lists are only helpful to "narrow the choices" a bit. We hope that we have met this intent with these fly selections for Alaska's sport fish.

Sheefish

Alaska Mary Ann	Gray Ghost
Alaskan Smolt	Maribou Muddler
Blue Smolt	N.W.O. Streamer
Coronation	Woolly Bugger
Flash Fly	Egg Sucking Zonker

Cutthroat Trout

Baby Needlefish	Iliamna Pinkie
Blue Smolt	Muddler Minnow
Gastineau Smolt	Pheasant Tail Nymph
Gold Ribbed Hare's Ear	Roselyn's Sand Lance
Humpy	Woolly Bugger

Lake Trout

Blue Smolt	Muddler
Egg Sucking Leech	Wool Head Sculpin
Gray Ghost	Woolly Bugger
Humpy	Egg Sucking Zonker
Lake Leech	

Arctic Char

Blue Smolt	Iliamna Pinkie
Bunny Fly	Little Chinook
Copper and Orange	Parr Fly
Egg Sucking Leech	Polar Shrimp
Gold-Ribbed Hare's Ear	Salmon Fry

Dolly Varden

Alevin	Glo-Bug
Babine Special	Iliamna Pinkie
Battle Creek	Micro Egg
Bunny Fly	Salmon Fry
Egg Sucking Leech	Woolly Bugger